The Parables
of
Dr. Seuss

Also by Robert L. Short

The Gospel According to Dogs
The Gospel According to Peanuts
The Gospel from Outer Space
The Parables of Peanuts
Short Meditations on the Bible and Peanuts
Something to Believe In
A Time to Be Born—A Time to Die

The Parables
of
Dr. Seuss

Robert L. Short

WESTMINSTER
JOHN KNOX PRESS
LOUISVILLE · KENTUCKY

Scripture quotations, unless otherwise indicated, are from the New Revised Standard Version of the Bible, copyright © 1989 by the Division of Christian Education of the National Council of the Churches of Christ in the U.S.A., and are used by permission.

Scripture quotations marked Moffatt are taken from James Moffatt, *A New Translation of the Bible, Containing the Old and New Testaments.* New York: Doran, 1926. Revised edition, New York and London: Harper and Brothers, 1935. Reprinted, Grand Rapids: Kregel, 1995.

Scripture quotations marked NEB are taken from *The New English Bible,* © The Delegates of the Oxford University Press and The Syndics of the Cambridge University Press, 1961, 1970. Used by permission.

Scripture quotations marked NJB are from *The New Jerusalem Bible,* copyright © 1985 by Darton, Longman & Todd, Ltd., and Doubleday, a division of Bantam Doubleday Dell Publishing Group, Inc. Reprinted by permission of the publisher(s).

Scripture quotations marked PHILLIPS are from *The New Testament in Modern English,* revised edition, translated by J. B. Phillips. © J. B. Phillips 1958, 1960, 1972. Used by permission of Macmillan Publishing Company.

Scripture quotations marked REB are taken from *The Revised English Bible,* © Oxford University Press and Cambridge University Press, 1989. Used by permission.

Scripture quotations marked RSV are from the Revised Standard Version of the Bible, copyright © 1946, 1952, 1971, and 1973 by the Division of Christian Education of the National Council of the Churches of Christ in the U.S.A., and are used by permission.

Book design by Drew Stevens
Cover illustration and design by RD Studio

First edition
Published by Westminster John Knox Press
Louisville, Kentucky

This book is printed on acid-free paper that meets the American National Standards Institute Z39.48 standard. ∞

08 09 10 11 12 13 14 15 16 17 — 10 9 8 7 6 5 4 3 2

Library of Congress Cataloging-in-Publication Data

Short, Robert L.
    The parables of Dr. Seuss / Robert L. Short.—1st ed.
        p. cm.
    ISBN 978-0-664-23047-0 (alk. paper)
    1. Seuss, Dr.—Religion.   2. Christianity and literature—United States—History—
20th century.   I. Title.
    PS3513.E2Z85   2008
    813'.52—dc22
    [B]   2007031685

For two very classy ladies in my life:

Alice always.

*And also for my sister, Helen, who I am sure is
as wonderful as was the Helen in Dr. Seuss's life!*

Contents

Introduction:
The Use and Abuse of Dr. Seuss

The use of Dr. Seuss begins when we make use of his beautifully imaginative stories to entertain our children. "You have
'em, I'll amuse 'em," the good Doctor, himself childless, would
often say.[1] The abuse of Dr. Seuss begins when that's all we use
him for. In *Moby Dick* Herman Melville tells us, "The man that
has anything bountifully laughable about him, be sure there is
more in that man than you perhaps think for."[2] Use of Dr.
Seuss appreciates the laughter in his work; abuse of Dr. Seuss is
to think that there's little more than laughter to appreciate.

Theodor Seuss Geisel's first career goal was a professorship in
English literature. As soon as this English major graduated from
Dartmouth College in 1925, he set out to earn a doctorate in
English at Oxford University. But it didn't take him long to find
the faculty at Oxford to be much too stuffy and humorless for his
taste. He then took off for Vienna to study modern German
drama. This also didn't suit him, so he finally ended up at the Sorbonne in Paris, where he hoped to do a dissertation on Jonathan
Swift. However, his professors along this path didn't satisfy him
either, so he returned to the United States and yielded to what he
knew he loved without question—he married Helen Palmer.

I mention these early attempts at serious sophisticated literary study merely to introduce a few important things often overlooked about Ted Geisel: he was well-educated, extremely intelligent, and evidentially possessed a depth that he never cared to wear on his sleeve. In their biography of Dr. Seuss, Judith and Neil Morgan claim that "much of the time he didn't think of himself as a children's book author."[3] The laughter was always there, but at the same time there was always much "more in that man than you perhaps think for."

Today it would seem we still see only a surface Seuss. What we get when grownups write about him is usually along the lines of what Dr. Seuss himself called "bunny-bunny" tripe.[4] That is, he was "everyone's inner child"; he was "the master of the batty and wacky, the lord of the goony and loony," the "creator of inspired lunacy," and so forth. In other words, cotton candy cuteness. Fun, fluff, and frivolity along with an occasional commonplace moral lesson, we are left to understand, is about all we can expect from this man who himself abhorred the "cute."[5]

As Dr. Seuss's fame and financial success grew to mammoth proportions, with staggering sales of his rapidly increasing number of book titles, one might wonder if he didn't finally achieve everything he could have wanted. But this wasn't the case. Not only did money tend to bore him, but apparently he longed for some recognition of the deeper dimension in his work. In the Morgans' biography, *Dr. Seuss and Mr. Geisel*, this yearning is clearly described in the obvious disappointment Ted Geisel experienced following the opening of an impressive retrospective exhibition of his work, a show collected in 1986 at the San Diego Museum of Art. The director of the museum found that on this occasion Ted Geisel continued to be "starved for somebody . . . who understood what he was trying to do [as an artist] and did not see him solely as a children's author, a Disney or a Jim Henson, the children's entrepreneurs with whom he was being compared."[6] It was also the superficial and shallow that the good Doctor believed today's children needed far less of. In 1987 he told *Parents* magazine:

There was a time when I thought [TV] would stimulate kids' minds—it still does, and I think they have a breadth of understanding, but not a depth of understanding. They know more things that are going on in the world, but not what the hell they're about.[7]

I well remember my first reading of his 1973 book *Did I Ever Tell You How Lucky You Are?* I thought, "What is this? Existentialism for children? Exiseussialism?" In a 1972 interview with *Newsweek*, Geisel was asked if he was "happy with his role as Dr. Seuss," to which he replied, "Nobody's really happy about anything."[8] "Good grief," I thought. "This sounds more like Albert Cameuss than Dr. Seuss!" Nevertheless, spoiled children—including adult spoiled children—would seem to have little use for anything smacking of "depth." And it's this attitude that makes for abuse of Seuss—the neglecting of a deeper Dr. Seuss.

I'm sure that part of the proper use of Seuss involves taking him more seriously as an artist. But I'm not prepared to say what this means, being neither an artist nor an art critic. But as one who prowls among a lot of theological thinking, I can see much in Dr. Seuss that has been overlooked. A close examination of his work through the lens of Christian faith can lead to some amazing graces. When I first became acquainted with his books and was struck by the many parallels I saw between his work and what is said in the Bible and by Christian faith, I considered these similarities to be merely "happy accidents." Today I still see these parallels as "happy," but I am now convinced that they are not merely "accidents." In this book I tend to argue that Ted Geisel was a first-class Christian thinker and that this thinking was intentionally made part of the literary and artistic work he has given us.

But did Dr. Seuss himself ever publicly say that he had incorporated in his work his own Christian faith? No, and as an artist he should not have. Why? Because art—unless it is to become mere propaganda—never tells us anything except artistically or indirectly. If the artist "gives away" what he's saying by saying it directly, then why be an artist? Also, it's only in this way that the right kind of discussion can take place—that is, an earnest discussion that will always continue and in which

the participants themselves must decide on the truth of the
matter. The artist places in a work of faith an element that will
usually be recognized only by the eyes of faith. Faith then
points this element out. Nonfaith says, "Nonsense!" Thus, this
conversation begins and will always continue because the artist
himself has said nothing. But the idea is that in this very discussion itself, nonfaith may learn a few things it has never
known before. Or as Dr. Seuss once said in another context,
"You have to sneak up on them."[9]

But surely this must be frustrating to the artist himself to
have something to say that he's so concerned about and yet not
being able to say it openly, and therefore running the risk of
constantly being misunderstood. No doubt this is frustrating,
and no doubt also that this is one of the prices artists must pay
for being so good at getting our attention. But if my hunch is
right that Dr. Seuss was profoundly Christian in his orientation,
then he must have found great comfort in Paul's belief that

> the good that people do can be obvious; but even when it
> is not, it cannot remain hidden.
>
> (1 Tim. 5:25 NJB)

This technique of a "hidden truth" is one Jesus used in his
parables. As one New Testament commentator has written
about the parables of Jesus, "If God hides anything, it is with
the purpose of ultimately revealing it; the temporary hiding is
itself part of the total process of revelation—a profound view of
the ways of God with men."[10] Or as Jesus himself said about
the element of mystery in his parables,

> there is nothing hid, except to be made manifest; nor is
> anything secret, except to come to light.
>
> (Mark 4:22 RSV)

In any case, I have always enjoyed putting the parallels I see
between Dr. Seuss and Christian faith to what I consider "good
use." As a Christian, this is what I believe Jesus has commanded me to do: "What I say to you in the dark you must
repeat in broad daylight; what you hear whispered you must

shout from the housetops" (Matt. 10:27 REB). And so I use
these parallels as "parables of the kingdom of God."

Parables are analogies from popular culture designed to
teach, just as the parables of Jesus are analogies from popular
culture (his own culture) designed to teach his own message—
"the Christian message." This is why this book is called *The
Parables of Dr. Seuss*. For in this book I want to use Dr. Seuss's
stories fully—as I believe they were designed to be used.

Charles Schulz always told me that he was "flattered" to see
Peanuts used this way—"as inspirational background for spiritual
thinking," to use his words—and always encouraged me to do so.
So for years now, along with my *Peanuts* slides I usually take my
Dr. Seuss slides with me on visits to churches and schools and
elsewhere to help me talk about the good news of the kingdom of
God. And I know from experience that these parables do help—
they "work." So, for instance, I am the one who is flattered when
someone says to me after a program, "You have really deepened
my appreciation of Dr. Seuss," or better still, "You have really
increased my understanding of the Christian message."

As it happens, *Peanuts* and Dr. Seuss go together very well.
Although Schulz and Geisel never met, I had the opportunity
to meet Dr. Seuss very briefly when he was in Chicago in 1978
on a book-signing tour. I found him to be, just as I had expected,
an amiable and kind man. I sent him copies of my books *The
Gospel According to Peanuts* and *The Parables of Peanuts* soon
after that meeting, and in reply he wrote,

> Thank you very much for giving me the pleasure of read-
> ing the *Gospel* and the *Parables of Peanuts*. I am a great
> admirer of Charlie Schulz and enjoyed the way you han-
> dled the material.[11]

I hope he also would have enjoyed the way I've "handled the
material" of this book.

When Ted Geisel was a student at Oxford he proposed to
the Oxford University Press that they publish and he illustrate
a new popular edition of Milton's masterpiece of Christian
poetry, *Paradise Lost*.[12] But the brilliance behind this suggestion was lost on the Oxford people and they turned him down.

My feeling is that Dr. Seuss never really got over this snub and therefore became determined that someday he would write his own brand of popular Christian poetry and illustrate it himself! So we hope this book will raise at least two questions in readers' minds: First, isn't something very much like this really what Dr. Seuss was saying? And second, regardless of what Dr. Seuss was saying, isn't this exactly what the New Testament is saying? Jesus would usually introduce his questions by asking, "What do you think?" (For example, Matthew 16:15, 17:25, 18:12, 21:28, etc.) In this way people would have to think for themselves and decide for themselves.

For extensive help with this book, I owe gratitude heaped on gratitude to gentle lady Alice Buckley for her kind and expert assistance in every way, and to my editor at Westminster John Knox Press, the dauntless David Dobson, who never stopped believing in this project.

Notes

1. Quoted in E. J. Kahn Jr., "Children's Friend," *New Yorker*, December 17, 1960, 47.

2. Herman Melville, *Moby Dick* (New York: Modern Library, 1950), 29.

3. Judith and Neil Morgan, *Dr. Seuss and Mr. Geisel: A Biography* (New York: Random House, 1995), 213.

4. Kahn, "Children's Friend, 86.

5. Ibid.

6. Morgan, *Dr. Seuss and Mr. Geisel*, 267.

7. Quoted in Michael J. Blander, "Seuss on the Loose," *Parents*, September 1987, 118.

8. Quoted in Martin Karindorf, "A Happy Accident," *Newsweek*, February 21, 1972, 74.

9. Quoted in David Dempsey, "The Significance of Dr. Seuss," *New York Times Book Review*, May 11, 1958.

10. Frederick C. Grant, "Exegesis of the Gospel According to St. Mark," *Interpreter's Bible*, vol. 7 (Nashville: Abingdon Press, 1951), 702.

11. Letter of Theodor S. Geisel to Robert Short, November 5, 1978.

12. Kahn, "Children's Friend," 61.

1

Difficult to Stomach:
"My Body and Blood"
and Green Eggs and Ham

When Hamlet gives the "players" some advice about the art of acting, he tells them that their job is to "suit the action to the word, the word to the action" (3.2). Now Dr. Seuss's stories do a masterful job of suiting their actions to their words, their words to their actions. But it's very often the case that his stories also "suit the action to the Word." And by "the Word" here I mean that his stories very often suit or "fit" the Word of the Christian message in marvelously surprising and closely analogous ways. They can be seen and understood as brand-new parables of the kingdom.

And it's for this reason that they give me, and people like me, the opportunity to "suit the Word to the action"—that is, to attempt to explain the Word of God in words and images that are easier for folks to grasp and understand—like Dr. Seuss's words and images, for example. We don't want to do violence either to the Dr. Seuss story or to the Word of God. But whenever it's possible, and it very often is, we want to suit the Dr. Seuss story to the God story, the God story to the Dr. Seuss story, to go back to Hamlet's way of putting it.

Theodor "Dr. Seuss" Geisel. Photo courtesy of Robert Short

Could Dr. Seuss have intended these things? Sure, he could have. There are many things we know about Theodor Seuss Geisel that might suggest that he wasn't always as innocent of putting things between the lines as he so frequently claimed. But then just about all artists make this kind of claim. "I have no hidden messages; I do no between-the-lines preaching!" they tell us. But what should we expect them to say? As artists, their job is to communicate indirectly, or artistically, not directly or bluntly, as with us plain, blunt preachers. Dr. Seuss has gone on record saying things like:

I get away with preaching by disguising the message.[1]

But that still doesn't mean his "message" is anything like the message that I see his stories being so well suited to. Ted Geisel was a well-educated man. He came from a middle-class Connecticut family, German Protestant in background, and in 1925 graduated from Dartmouth, where he studied English literature. Later on he pursued graduate studies in literature at Oxford and then at the Sorbonne, in Paris. While at Oxford he tried to talk the Oxford University Press into publishing a new edition of Milton's *Paradise Lost*, which he himself would illustrate. One of the drawings he proposed was "to show the Archangel Uriel sliding down a sunbeam with a long-necked oilcan in his hand, to slick his passage."[2] No wonder they didn't understand him at Oxford! Nevertheless, Dr. Seuss's early and not too slick passage from Oxford notwithstanding, his ambition was still for a professorship in English literature and so to become a "Dr." in the PhD sense. And it was only his strong addiction to eating that forced him to change directions and choose a career that provided at least enough revenue to put food on the table.

But the point is that Dr. Seuss certainly *could* have intended all sorts of subtle things that we don't see on the surface of his stories. Schooled in literature, he knew how literary artists— including the writers of the Bible—had always done this kind of thing. But was Dr. Seuss himself intent on communicating something to us on a much deeper level, something that we don't usually recognize in his stories? He once said,

> There is no particular message in these books, unless it's one of eternal hope.[3]

He also said,

> I've been accused of being the greatest moralist since Elsie Dinsmore, but I don't believe it. If you write any sort of drama . . . the reader can impute a moral into it.[4]

So, then, I suggest we take him at his word and leave it at that. Or rather, leave the job of "in-putting" morals to preachers like me. One way or another, Dr. Seuss has suited the action to the Word. My job, as a preacher, is very intentionally to suit the Word to Dr. Seuss's "actions." So please,

If the shoe fits, wear it.

Or to put it another way,

If the parable preaches, hear it.

Now *Green Eggs and Ham* is probably the most popular of all of Dr. Seuss's stories. Parents the world over read it to their children until they're green in the face. I know this from the experience of having turned somewhat green myself a couple of times. And then these children read it to their children, and so on and on and on. Actually, I don't think I need to read it any more. I think I now have the whole thing memorized, like Zoe in *Baby Blues*.

 Baby Blues   Rick Kirkman & Jerry Scott

© Baby Blues Partnership. King Features Syndicate

But there are many, many much worse things that could be built into our heads like this. T. S. Eliot was no doubt right in saying that mostly nowadays our "headpieces are filled with straw." But I consider *Green Eggs and Ham* far more substantial than straw. And that's primarily because there's so much about *Green Eggs and Ham* that parallels what Jesus and the New Testament have to say. Dr. Seuss or Mr. Geisel has told us:

> More ministers use [*Green Eggs and Ham*] in their sermons than any other book of mine. They find the damnedest things in it.[5]

I'm just one of those ministers. I find the damnedest things in *Green Eggs and Ham*.

For instance, look at how much Jesus and Sam-I-am have in common. Both of them are dead set on getting someone to eat something, something that they know can be very, very difficult to swallow. Now of course Jesus knew that everyone had to have something to eat in order to stay healthy and strong; he knew that everyone at least had to have bread, for example, which is probably the most common food in the world. But Jesus also knew that people don't "live by bread alone" (Matt. 4:4). He knew that people—all people—need something more than just plain old bread, or food, to make it through this life in the best and most perfectly fulfilled way. Jesus knew that all people also need him, need Jesus himself, to make it through life as they were originally designed to do. And so, then, Jesus said that he himself was that other food that all people need. In the prayer of Jesus, when we pray, "Give us this day our daily bread," we're asking God to give us not only the bread or food that makes our bodies strong, but we're also asking God to give us Jesus, that other kind of bread that makes our spirits strong. Jesus knows that our spirits would never be satisfied one little bit without him. And this is why he could say,

> I am that living bread which has come down from heaven: if anyone eats this bread he shall live forever. Moreover, the bread I will give is my own flesh; I give it for the life of the world.
>
> (John 6:51 NEB)

Does this mean we're supposed to eat the flesh of Jesus? Yuck! That doesn't sound like anything anyone would like. And yet, Jesus can make it sound even yuckier:

> I tell you, unless you eat the flesh of the son of Man and drink his blood you have no life in you. Whoever eats my flesh and drinks my blood possesses eternal life, and I will raise him up on the last day. My flesh is real food; my blood is real drink.
>
> (John 6:53–55 NEB)

Well, yuck and double-yuck!! We're supposed to eat Jesus' flesh *and* drink his blood? That sounds worse than green eggs and ham! As a matter of fact, a lot of people, when they originally heard Jesus say this, were just as turned off as Sam's friend was. Whether it's green eggs and ham or Jesus' flesh and blood, this doesn't sound like anything we're going to like:

> Many of [Jesus'] disciples on hearing it exclaimed, 'This is more than we can stomach!'
> (John 6:60 NEB)

But, of course, Jesus didn't mean that we're to eat his physical flesh or drink his literal blood. The flesh and blood Jesus, the man, no longer lives among us in the world but with his father in heaven. Jesus meant that we should believe in him. Because only when we believe in him does his spirit live in us. We're to believe that it was only in the flesh and blood Jesus that God revealed himself once and for all for all humankind. And this is why Jesus could say,

> I am the bread of life. Whoever comes to me shall never be hungry, and whoever believes in me shall never be thirsty.
> (John 6:35 NEB)

There's an old saying that goes, "The proof of the pudding is in the eating." In other words, we're never going to know whether we like something or not until we try it. Just like Sam's friend, he didn't really know he didn't like green eggs and ham until he'd tried them. You probably remember what happened; he finally gives in:

> If you will let me be,
> I will try them.

And then:

> Say!
> I like green eggs and ham!

But you know, it's a strange thing—just like people aren't going to try something as yucky as green eggs and ham until they have to, people aren't going to believe in Jesus until they have to. And this is because no one in this world originally believes in Jesus. We all start out believing in something else. So this something else has got to be let go of or washed away before we can believe in Jesus. No one can really believe in Jesus until they become aware of their need. No one is going to clean up their lives very much until they first find themselves in hot water, about like Sam-I-am's friend who finally almost drowns trying to avoid eating green eggs and ham. And this is why the New Testament tells us that baptism is a way of describing what we've all got to go through before we can really believe in Jesus:

> Have you forgotten that when we were baptized into union with Christ Jesus we were baptized into his death? By baptism we were buried with him, and lay dead, in order that, as Christ was raised from the dead in the splendor of the Father, so also we might set our feet upon the new path of life.
> (Rom. 6:3–4 NEB)

Only when we're forced to do it, when we really need to do it, will we really try Jesus. It's not until we get ourselves into a big enough stew that we'll actually swallow a food that all of us just naturally don't think we care for. No, by nature we just don't think we like them at all—Jesus and green eggs and ham. If only they looked more appealing or appetizing.

But just as we don't think we like green eggs and ham because of the way it looks, Jesus is likewise careful not to provide us with any showy things about himself to appeal to us. Otherwise, he realizes, we're going to end up more devoted to the "show business" than to him. Just as we turn up our noses at green eggs and ham because it looks so ridiculous and yucky, Jesus doesn't dress himself up as all provable reasonableness or flashy supernatural solicitings either. He wants us to swallow him, not them. But then when we do swallow Jesus, the food from heaven, we're just like Sam-I-am's friend, shouting, "Thank you! Thank you, Sam-I-am!"

© Mark Parisi/Dist. by United Feature
Syndicate, Inc.

And so *Green Eggs and Ham* ends in the very same way that
it begins, with that crazy name that only Dr. Seuss could have
thought of: "Sam-I-am." Or maybe this name isn't so crazy
after all. "Sam" is short for Samuel, and Samuel is the Old Testament name that means "name of God." And what is God's
name in the Old Testament? It's "I AM." God's name is the Old
Testament is "I AM"!?!? That's right. You may remember how it
happened:

> Moses said to God, "If I come to the Israelites and say to
> them, 'The God of your ancestors has sent me to you,' and
> they ask me 'What is his name?' what shall I say to them?"
> God said to Moses, "I AM WHO I AM. . . . Thus you shall say
> to the Israelites, 'I AM has sent me to you.'"
>
> (Exod. 3:13–14)

But then how is all of this related to Jesus? Well, I think the
tentative or incomplete nature of God's answer here to Moses
is pretty obvious: "My name is 'I AM.'" But now, God, what do
you mean by that? Who am you? What am you? Where am

you? Well, it was precisely to complete God's revelation of himself and to answer these still unanswered questions that Jesus came into the world. This is why in the Gospel of John, Jesus can hardly say often enough who "he am":

> Jesus said, "I am the bread of life . . . the light of the world . . . the gate for the sheep . . . the good shepherd . . . the way, the truth, and the life . . . the resurrection and the life . . . the true vine . . ."

That, exactly, is who and where and what God "am"—he *am* Jesus the Lord. And so it's just this Sam-I-am himself in the fullest and most complete sense who offers us all something we don't think we're going to like to swallow—until we try it. It's just this Sam-I-am himself who says to us,

> I am the bread of life. . . . I am that living bread which has come down from heaven.
>
> (John 6:48, 51 NEB)

So to follow him is to swallow him. And if we do follow/swallow Jesus, we'll always say—always—and again and again:

> Thank you!
> Thank you,
> Sam-I-am!

Notes

1. Quoted in Diane Roback, "Coming Attractions," *Publishers Weekly,* February 23, 1990, 126.

2. E. J. Kahn Jr., "Children's Friend," *New Yorker,* December 17, 1960, 61.

3. Quoted in David Dempsey, "The Significance of Dr. Seuss," *New York Times Book Review,* May 11, 1958.

4. "Ted 'Dr. Seuss' Geisel," in Digby Diehl, *Supertalk;* (New York: Doubleday, 1974), 169.

5. Roback, "Coming Attractions."

2

Oh, the Places Christians Will Go!

> Although I am the very least of all the saints, this grace was given to me to bring to the Gentiles the news of the boundless riches of Christ, and to make everyone see what is the plan of the mystery hidden for ages by God who created all things; so that through the church the wisdom of God in its rich variety might now be made known to the rulers and authorities in the heavenly places. This was in accordance with the eternal purpose that he has carried out in Christ Jesus our Lord, in whom we have access to God in boldness and confidence through faith in him. I pray therefore that I may not lose heart over my sufferings for you; they are your glory.
>
> —Eph. 3:8–13

When theologian Dietrich Bonhoeffer was in Berlin's Tegel Prison in 1944, he wrote to his friend Eberhard Bethge that he had been reading a study of the ancient gods of Greece; and that these gods, as far removed from Christ as they obviously were, nevertheless were in some ways closer to Christ than many modern-day points of view that proudly proclaim themselves to be "true Christianity." "These gods" . . . when they are so treated," says Bonhoeffer, "[are] less offensive than certain brands of Christianity. . . . I almost think I could claim these gods for Christ."[1]

In much the same way, this is how I feel about Dr. Seuss and his stories. Ted Geisel certainly never boasted of being any kind of super-Christian. Yet his stories—and his life—often exhibit a greater nearness to Christ than those who do. So treated, his stories are indeed less offensive than certain brands of Christianity and therefore I almost think we can claim these stories for Christ. Let's take *Oh, the Places You'll Go!* for example. "Congratulations!" it begins. "You're off to Great Places!" "Congratulations!" for what? We're not told. It could be a graduation of some kind, or maybe the beginning of a new job with new opportunities on the horizon. All we know is that something very new and promising has happened in a person's life, and now that person is really going to go places. "Oh, the places you'll go!" And so begins this person's journey, a journey that is a "rich variety" if nothing else. There is never a dull moment—never an uncolorful page, an unimaginatively drawn scene, a situation without hope and excitement. There is always a "rich variety."

Now it would be very easy to hold this book in one hand and leaf through the Bible with the other and spot all sorts of similar-to-Seuss things. This is because the Bible contains such a rich variety also. But there is one little spot in the Bible that seems to wrap up just about everything Dr. Seuss is saying in this story. In fact, there are probably several. But the one that jumps out at me is one of the few places in the New Testament that talks about the "places" where Christians will go.

Christians believe they'll go to heaven, of course. And so apparently did Dr. Seuss. Not long before he died he could still remember a verse he'd composed some fifty years earlier, which he called "I Am Prepared":

> When I cross the Bar of the Great Blue Beyonder
> I know that my Maker, without pause or ponder,
> Will welcome my soul. For my record is scar-less
> I've eaten no oysters in months that are R-less.[2]

These wouldn't seem to be the words of someone who took himself with a heavy dose of gloomy seriousness or was at all worried about not being welcome in the Great Blue Beyond. And as Charles Schulz once pointed out, there's a close connection between humor and faith:

> "Humor is a proof of faith, proof that everything is going to be all right with God, nevertheless."[3]

But in one of the rare places in the New Testament that talks about the "places" where Christians can expect to go, Paul is not talking about the "heaven" of the ultimate future. As we'll see a little bit later, Paul fully believes that finally *everyone* will go to heaven. But right now he's talking about where Christians—"the church"—can expect to go "now," in this lifetime. And he also talks of these places in terms of a "rich variety":

> so that through the church the wisdom of God in its rich variety might now be made known to the rulers and authorities in the heavenly places.
>
> (Eph. 3:10)

For Paul, evidently Christians could actually expect to make it to places beyond the boundaries of this world. It almost sounds as if Paul fully expects Christians to someday become the Luke Skywalkers of the universe—to walk among the "heavenly places."

But why would Christians want to go to such out-of-the-way places? Because they have a mission—they have a message to carry to literally "everyone." Here's the way Paul sums up the Christian's grand tour of the universe:

> Although I am the very least of all the saints, this grace was given to me to bring to the Gentiles the news of the boundless riches of Christ, and to make everyone see what is the plan of the mystery hidden for ages by God who created all things; so that through the church the wisdom of God in its rich variety might now be made known to the rulers and authorities in the heavenly places.
>
> (Eph. 3:8–10)

"Oh, the places you'll go!" Paul is saying to the church, the company of Christ's followers.

And when Dr. Seuss likewise tells us of the places we'll go, there are remarkable similarities between his way of looking at the matter and Paul's. In any case, Dr. Seuss furnishes us with an illuminating and charming modern analogue for much of what Paul is saying, especially in his letter to the Ephesians, and it may be that Paul can even shed light on Dr. Seuss.

In the first place (among all these "places"), both of these men knew their lives were drawing to a close. Scholars tell us that Ephesians was among the last things that Paul wrote, if not the last, and biographers of Dr. Seuss assure us that "there was never any doubt that Ted considered *Oh, The Places You'll Go!* his farewell salute, his last parade."[4] So then it's not surprising that in both of these works we hear a sort of summing up, along with a final bit of wisdom for probably the last group of "graduates" that either of these men would be addressing.

The hero of Dr. Seuss's story even resembles Paul—Paul the *small* (as the name "Paul" means), a child of faith, "the very least of all the saints." And he's immediately told by the creator of this story, as Paul is told by his creator, to get moving, to get on his way. And Paul the Jew is no sooner converted to faith in Christ than he's also informed by his Lord that his mission will not be among his own people but to the non-Jews, or to the "Gentiles," as the New Testament refers to non-Jews. Probably Paul could have come to this conclusion all by himself, since his original attempts to spread Christian faith among the Jews were met with an understandable hostility—a hostility reserved for turncoats like Paul. Not only that but Paul also found the avenues of the Jews, or their "law," to be much too straight and rigid, much too lacking in opportunities for creativity and freedom and in the flexibility of forgiveness. And so Paul, just like the little guy in Dr. Seuss's story, rejects the forbidding and stern streets he starts out from and instead heads straight out of town into "the wide-open air"; or as Paul describes this in Ephesians, "In Christ we have access to God with freedom" (3:12 NEB).

And so Paul and his lookalike become travel-airs *extraordinaire*. They start going places. And just as soon as they set out, both are told of what Kierkegaard would call "the gospel of suffering." Dr. Seuss expresses this "good news" by saying that things can happen even

> to people as brainy
> and footsy as you.

But we shouldn't worry, he continues, because eventually

> *You'll* start happening too.

Paul also was certainly a brainy and footsy foot soldier for Christ to whom a lot of things started happening. And he was also told not to worry, for he would "start happening too." Or, as God actually said to Paul,

> My grace is sufficient for you; for my power is made perfect in weakness.
>
> (2 Cor. 12:9)

Much of the message that both Paul and Dr. Seuss are passing along to us in these two works deals with the kind of mission we must be on if we really expect to go places. In this sense "the mission is the message." They both seem to be saying, "To get lots of mileage, you must have a great mission. If you really want to go great places, then you've got to have something great to go for. The greater the goal, the farther you'll go." Furthermore, if you really want to be unconquerable in this quest, if you want to be a winner no matter what happens, then what you are going for must also be unconquerable. It must already be the winner.

Paul makes this very clear when he tells us that the mission he's on is also the mission of the entire church: ". . . so that through the church the wisdom of God in its rich variety might now be made known to the rulers and authorities in the heavenly places" (Eph. 3:10). He, and the whole church with him, have been sent "to bring . . . the news of the boundless riches of Christ, and to make everyone see what is the plan of the mystery hidden for ages by God who created all things" (3:8–9). With this kind of mission, there is no way that Christians can finally fail: "We are more than conquerors through him who loved us," Paul says in Romans 8:37.

That's the mission of the saints. But what's the mission of the Dr. Seuss-man? It would seem to be similar, if not identical. His mission is to "move mountains":

> Your mountain is waiting.
> So . . . *get on your way!*

And where does this phrase "moving mountains" come from? It comes from Jesus, of course, who first presented us with this startling image when he said:

> If you have faith the size of a mustard seed, you will say to this mountain, "Move from here to there," and it will move.
>
> (Matt. 17:20)

And what does Jesus mean by "moving mountains"? Shall we hold Jesus to an unimaginative literalism and doubt him because we know we've had good faith and yet no honest-to-goodness mountain has ever done any jumping around for us? Was Jesus really so one-dimensional in his use of words that we're supposed to read the Gospels like we'd read the fine print of a life insurance policy? No, of course not. Jesus was the master of metaphor; he was a skillful poet or literary artist who could pack meaning into his words at many different levels at one time. So back to our question: What does Jesus mean by "moving mountains"?

As always, the best way to interpret a specific passage in the New Testament is with other things the New Testament says. And Jesus constantly talks about the horribly heavy burdens people carry around with them as long as they don't follow him and hence don't carry him in their hearts. For instance, he could say:

> Come to me, all you that are weary and are carrying heavy burdens, and I will give you rest.
>
> (Matt. 11:28)

Let's try this same verse in other words:

> Come to me, all you that are weary and are carrying a mountain around on your back, and I will toss that mountain into the sea.
>
> (Dr. Short)

Jesus could make these personal, heart-crushing mountains of ours move. On the other hand,

> The scribes and the Pharisees . . . tie up heavy burdens, hard
> to bear, and lay them on the shoulders of others; but they
> themselves are unwilling to lift a finger to move them.
>
> (Matt. 23:2, 4)

So when Jesus said that faith could move mountains, he was no
more talking about a merely physical reality than we are when
we say, "He has the weight of the world on his shoulders." Jesus
was primarily concerned about spiritual things, not physical
things. We are not talking about physical disabilities when we
say that the job of Christians is to remove scales from people's
eyes, hardness from their hearts, mountains off their backs, and
stains from their souls.

Likewise the job of Dr. Seuss's little man is to move mountains. But no one said this would be easy—neither Dr. Seuss
nor Paul nor Jesus. Dr. Seuss tells us that

> Bang-ups
> and Hang-ups
> can happen to you.

He also warns us that there will be times when we will play
"lonely games,"

> Games you can't win 'cause you'll play against you.

How much this sounds like Paul—up against himself:

> I pray therefore that I may not lose heart over my sufferings
> for you; they are your glory.
>
> (Eph. 3:13)

It's also possible to get so confused that we end up at the horrible
"Waiting Place"! And what's so bad about "The Waiting Place?"

> People are just waitin',
> They have no mission.
> They're just standin' there starin',
> Or sittin' or fishin.' (Dr. Short)

So whether we are talking about "Christian" in Bunyan's *Pilgrim's Progress*, or the nameless little pilgrim in Dr. Seuss's *Oh, the Places You'll Go!* or just the pilgrimage of the ordinary Christian, there will always be plenty of problems to be faced. But both Dr. Seuss and Paul tell us to hike confidently as far as we need to face up to our problems. And will we succeed? Yes! We will indeed! "98 and 3/4 percent guaranteed." But how can we be so sure? Because the outcome has already been decided, an outcome we know through faith in Christ:

> This was in accordance with the eternal purpose that [God] has carried out in Christ Jesus our Lord, in whom we have access to God in boldness and confidence through faith in him.
>
> (Eph. 3:11–12)

All Christians are on a mission that is the only mission that finally can never fail—the mission of moving mountains for Christ:

> And to make everyone see what is the plan of the mystery hidden for ages by God who created all things.
>
> (Eph. 3:9)

But just what is this "hidden mystery"? What is this "secret" that we are supposed to help reveal? Paul tells us in Ephesians what this secret is. But does he also tell about the places where we will go and that we'll be on a mission that finally can't be defeated? Indeed he does! Just listen!

> God has made known to us his secret purpose in accordance with the plan which he determined beforehand in Christ, to be put into effect when the time was ripe: namely, that the universe, everything in heaven and on earth, might be brought into a unity in Christ.
>
> (Eph. 1:9–10 REB)

In case you missed it, Paul here makes it unmistakably clear where *everything*—including all people, Christians and non-

Christians alike—will finally go: "everything" will be "brought into a unity in Christ." And it's exactly this invincible plan that all Christians are "to make everyone see." This is what we're to move a mountain of ignorance and misunderstanding from. It's just this good news that Christians are to go and make known in their every word and deed. And it's just this God-given goal and in their striving to achieve it that assures Christians that they're on the right track and that they are for sure going to go places!

> You're off to Great Places!
> Today is your day!
> Your mountain is waiting.
> So . . . *get on your way!*

And oh the places you'll go!

Notes

1. Dietrich Bonhoeffer, *Letters and Papers from Prison*, new greatly enlarged ed. (New York: Macmillan, 1972), 333.

2. Quoted in Judith and Neil Morgan, *Dr. Seuss and Mr. Geisel* (New York: Random House, 1995), 273.

3. Quoted in Robert Short, *The Parables of Peanuts* (New York: Harper & Row, 1968), 145.

4. Morgan, *Dr. Seuss and Mr. Geisel*, 280.

3

A Cat in the Hat Catechism of Christian Faith

With Verses from the New Testament and Dr. Seuss's Hat-Haloed Cat

Question 1: What kind of person or people will catch on first to Christian faith?

Answer: A person or people who are like children, and are all alone.

Dr. Seuss: "So we sat in the house
All that cold, cold, wet day."

Jesus: "Truly I tell you, unless you change and become like children, you will never enter the kingdom of heaven" (Matt. 18:3).

Question 2: Who else is best suited for believing the Christian faith?

Answer: A person or a people who have nothing satisfying to do.

Dr. Seuss: "I sat there with Sally
We sat there we two.
And I said, 'How I wish
We had something to do!'

"So all we could do was to
Sit!"

Matthew: "The people who sat in darkness have seen a
great light" (4:16).

Jesus: "Blessed are the poor in spirit, for theirs is the
kingdom of heaven" (Matt. 5:3).

Question 3: When Christ, the Cat, the great light, opens
the door and comes into our lives, does he
come quietly and gently, or does he come
with a great BUMP?

Answer: No one can ever really be changed without
first experiencing a big foundation-shaking
BUMP!

Dr. Seuss: "Something went BUMP!
How that bump made us jump!"

Jesus: "In very truth I tell you, no one can see the
kingdom of God unless he has been born
again" (John 3:3 REB).

Question 4: Is there anything we do to bring the cat into
the house of our lives? Does the cat come
from within our own hearts?

Answer: No. The cat enters the house totally by his
own power and totally from outside in.

Dr. Seuss: "We did nothing at all."

Paul: "God . . . brought us to life with Christ even
when we were dead in our sins. . . . For it is
by his grace you are saved, through trusting
him; it is not your own doing. It is God's gift,
not a reward for work done. There is nothing
for anyone to boast of" (Eph. 2:5, 8–9 NEB).

Question 5: Why does Christ the Cat come into the world
and into our lives? Does he want to make us

feel guilty by giving us a bunch of rules and laws that no one can possibly keep? Does he want to frighten immature people with bugaboos like "hell" and "the devil"?

Answer: No. As Jesus said, "I came that they may have life, and have it abundantly" (John 10:10).

Dr. Seuss: "And we saw him!
The Cat in the Hat!
And he said to us,
'Why do you sit there like that? . . . We can have Lots of good fun that is funny!'"

Question 6: But doesn't Christian faith mean faith in the religious law?

Answer: No. Christian faith ultimately means faith in Christ, who alone could keep the religious law perfectly for us.

Paul: "For Christ is the end of the law and brings righteousness for everyone who has faith" (Rom. 10:4 REB).

Question 7: Then what should the Christian's attitude be toward the religious law?

Answer: The religious law is like the mother in the story of *The Cat in the Hat*. It was like a schoolmaster for Christians—a guardian and guide. But it is now no longer Christians' final guardian or guide. Their new guide they now find completely in Christ the Cat. (This is one reason Christians are called "Christians" and not "Lawyers.")

Dr. Seuss: The Cat then tells the children that he knows some "good games" that he and the children can play, as well as some "new tricks."

Paul: "Now before faith came, we were imprisoned and guarded under the law until faith would be revealed. Therefore the law was our disciplinarian until Christ came, so that we might be justified by faith. But now that faith has come, we are no longer subject to a disciplinarian, for in Christ Jesus you are all children of God through faith" (Gal. 3:23–26).

Question 8: In the story, the fish did not want the children to play with the Cat when their mother was not at home. Looks fishy, doesn't he? What about the fish in the story?

Answer: The fish is like the many churches and religious people that today still insist on living within the small and restricting bowl of some version of religious law.

Dr. Seuss: The fish is "my version of Cotton Mather" (a very restricting preacher in one of those churches).[1]

Paul: "While we were 'children' we lived under the authority of basic moral principles. But when the proper time came God sent his son . . . that he might redeem those who were under the authority of the law and lead us into becoming, by adoption, true sons of God. . . . Plant your feet firmly therefore within the freedom that Christ has won for us, and do not let yourselves be caught again in the shackles of slavery" (Gal. 4:3–5, 5:1, Phillips).

Question 9: Does faith in Christ then give Christians the freedom to ignore the law or to let it fall?

Answer: By no means. It upholds the law by placing it on a much firmer foundation. It replaces the law's authority with the greater authority of

	God and Christ, an authority that can be symbolized by a ball (or a "globe"), a book, and a cup.
Dr. Seuss:	Then the Cat tells the children not to fear his tricks, as they are not bad. He shows them one trick he calls "up-up-up with a fish!" He will not let the fish fall but will hold it up high as "I stand on a ball. With a book on one hand! And a cup on my hat!"
Paul:	"For our argument is that people are justified by faith quite apart from any question of keeping the law. . . . Does this mean that we are using faith to undermine the law? By no means: we are upholding the law" (Rom. 3:28, 31 REB).
Question 10:	Is our attitude toward the religious law the only thing that Christ revolutionizes?
Answer:	No. Christ revolutionizes our attitude toward everything. He shakes up the entire world. In his crucifixion, Christ begins this revolution by showing us once more the Old Testament's picture (in Gen. 3) of the original "fallenness" of all things.

Dr. Seuss: The Cat then begins to hop up and down on the ball while balancing a world of other things: two books, a little toy ship, some milk on a dish, a cake, the fish on a rake, a little toy man, and a red fan. But then the Cat falls on his head and all the things fall.

Matthew: "From noon on, darkness came over the whole earth. . . . Then Jesus cried again with a loud voice and breathed his last. At that moment the curtain of the temple was torn in two, from top to bottom. The earth shook, and the rocks were split" (27:45, 50–51).

Question 11:   How does Christ the Cat then continue his revolution of the world?

Answer: He shows us "something new: Two things," although these two new things are made from old things. These two new things are the "first" (Thing One) and "second" (Thing Two) commandments of the New Testament.

Dr. Seuss: The Cat assures the children that the two things he has in a box only want to have fun. "Then, out of the box / Came Thing Two and Thing One!"

Mark: "One of the scribes . . . asked him, 'Which commandment is the first of all?' Jesus answered, 'The first is, "Hear, O Isreal: the Lord our God, the Lord is one: you shall love the Lord your God with all your heart, and with all your soul, and with all your mind, and with all your strength." The second is this, "You shall love your neighbor as your-self." There is no other commandment greater than these'" (12:28–31).

Question 12: If the first commandment (Thing One) is actually a quotation from Deuteronomy 6:4 in the Old Testament, and the second commandment (Thing Two) is a quotation of Leviticus 19:18 in the Old Testament, why does Christ the Cat call these two things "something new"?

Answer: Thing One and Thing Two are new because they are now held together by the kite—that is, the cross of Christ—which gives our two merely human loves a power that neither of them have alone. Without the love of God that can be seen so clearly in Christ's cross, our weak and sinful loves would never get off the ground. This is why the cross-shape of the kites in *The Cat in the Hat* is so significant.[2] With-

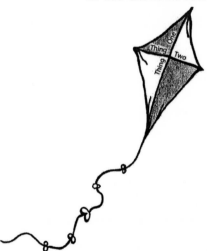

out being supported by the vertical dimension, the horizontal dimension—"Thing Two," or humanity's love for humanity—collapses and falls to the ground. Without being rooted and grounded in Christ and his love for us, the vertical dimension—"Thing One," or our love for God—also falls. It was no doubt Jesus who combined the first and second commandments into what he called the "greatest commandment" (Mark 12:31). Likewise, these two are never "something new" unless they are held firmly together by Christ and his cross.

Paul: "For while we were still weak, at the right time Christ died for the ungodly. . . . God proves his love for us in that while we still were sinners Christ died for us" (Rom. 5:6, 8).

Dr. Seuss: The Cat tells the fish and the children to have no fear, that the two Things are tame and only like to have fun.

Question 13: As we know from the story, Thing One and Thing Two at first shake hands with the children and then with their kites make a huge mess in the children's house. So is this the kind of result we can expect from the commandments of Christ the Cat when they are given their freedom "outside the box"?

Answer: Again, Christ the Cat will always be guilty of shaking everything up. The revolution of Christ the Cat will always turn everything upside down.

Luke: "They made for Jason's house, hoping to bring them before the People's Assembly; however, they found only Jason and some of the brothers, and these they dragged before the city council, shouting, 'The people who have been turning the whole world upside down have come here now. . . . They have broken Caesar's edicts by claiming that there is another king, Jesus'" (Acts 17:5–7 NJB).

Question 14: Just before the story ends and the children's mother returns, the children and the fish make Christ the Cat and his Two Things leave the house. Is there any way that alone the children and the fish can then clean up the

	"big mess" left behind by the Cat and his Two Things?
Answer:	No.
Dr. Seuss:	"There is no way at all," according to the fish.
Jesus:	"In the world you will have trouble" (John 16:33 NEB).

Question 15:	But is this answer the final answer, that "in the world you will have trouble," and that is that?
Answer:	No. For we know that quite unexpectedly the cat then comes back in the house. And he restores and cleans up everything. Totally! Completely! Leaving nothing or no one undone!
Jesus:	"I have told you all this so that in me you may find peace. In the world you will have trouble. but courage! The victory is mine; I have conquered the world" (John 16:33 NEB).

Question 16:	And now that we know this, what do we do?
Answer:	This is basically the question that Dr. Seuss seems to be asking at the end of the story. The children's mother comes home and asks them if they had any fun while she was gone. But they are not sure how to answer her. And then Dr. Seuss asks:

> What would YOU do
> If your mother asked YOU?

These are the final words of the story. And so in direct words alone the story's final question isn't answered—the question of "Now that we know this, what do we do?"

Dr. Seuss: But Dr. Seuss would seem to have given us his answer. For in this story he seems to be bearing his testimony in his own way. Through his art, he has evidently passed on to us a message that he himself has heard and so in this way advises us to do the same. The New Testament also advises us to do the same in its testament to "Christ the Cat."

John: "It was there from the beginning; we have heard it; we have seen it with our own eyes; we looked upon it, and felt it with our own hands; and it is of this we tell. Our theme is the word of life. This life was made visible; we have seen it and bear our testimony; we here declare to you the eternal life which dwelt with the Father and was made visible to us. . . . And we write this in order that the joy of us all may be complete. Here is the message we heard from him and pass on to you: that God is light, and in him there is no darkness at all" (1 John 1:1–2, 4–5 NEB).

Question 17: So finally, what is the good news that we learn from the Cat in the Hat?

Answer: "That God is light, and in him there is no darkness at all," and that furthermore we can be absolutely sure that this good news is true just as soon as that fun-loving, light-hearted Cat, Christ, comes into the house of our lives and completely takes over.

Notes

1. Quoted in Jonathan Cott, "The Good Dr. Seuss," *Of Sneetches and Whos and the Good Dr. Seuss: Essays on the Writings and Life of*

Theodor Geisel, ed. Thomas Feusch (Jefferson, NC: McFarland & Co., 1997), 116.

2. The cross in the conventional kite form has evidently been widely used as a Christian symbol. For instance, in Bermuda there is a tradition of flying kites on Good Friday, to represent Christ's ascension into heaven following the crucifixion.

4

The Christian Parable
of The Lorax

Among all of Dr. Seuss's stories, *The Lorax* is probably the best example of how the good Doctor could give us two kinds of good at the same time—the obvious good and the hidden good. We remember Paul's statement to Timothy:

> . . . . the good that people do can be obvious; but even when it is not, it cannot remain hidden.
>
> (1 Tim. 5:25 NJB)

And so people commenting on *The Lorax* have generally fastened on its obvious good—its lessons about good environmental practices—and they have walked away from the story apparently feeling that it has little more of importance to tell us. The story is seen primarily as a morality tale, a cautionary preachment about pollution and conservation and corporate greed. These are the story's obvious goods, its moral goods, a knowledge requiring nothing related to revelation. Or, as Horatio could say to his friend Hamlet, "There needs no ghost, my lord, come from the grave/To tell us this" (1.5.124).

But doesn't *The Lorax* go deeper than this? Is there not something in it beyond these obvious moral lessons, something that remains hidden? I think so. In the first place, such a one-dimensional merely moral interpretation leaves far more questions about the story than it bothers to answer. For example, as the story's narrator himself asks:

> What *was* the Lorax?
> And why was it there?
> And why was it lifted and taken somewhere . . . ?

Our problem would seem to be that it never occurs to us to look more deeply into Dr. Seuss.

> If you look deep enough you can still see, today,
> where the Lorax once stood
> just as long as it could
> before somebody lifted the Lorax away.

Who was this "somebody" who "lifted the Lorax away"? And why? Where does the Lorax's peculiar name come from? And the name of the other central figure in the story, "The Once-ler"—what's that all about? And—

> those thees! Those *trees!*
> *Those Truffula trees!*
> All my life I'd been searching
> For trees such as these.

What's behind those trees? Why is "Truffula" so special? At the very end of the story when the Once-ler tosses the tiny Truffula seed—"the last one of all!"—to the story's unnamed narrator, he calls out to the boy, "Catch!" And so it would seem that most of the meaning of this story—like this seed we see in the story's final picture—still remains up in the air for us to catch.

As I see it, most of the hidden elements in the story are closely related to Scripture. This in itself is likely to be surprising, as we don't ordinarily think of Dr. Seuss as thinking all that much about Scripture. After all, wasn't Dr. Seuss simply an artist and a writer of charming books for children? So what should we expect him to know about the contents of the Bible? But we should be disabused of this kind of prejudice. I am reminded here of Handel, who gave us his masterful *Messiah*. In 1737 when Queen Caroline of England died and Handel was asked to compose her funeral anthem, the Anglican bishop of London offered Handel, a mere "layman," his help in selecting passages of Scripture for the anthem. But Handel gruffly told the bishop, "I have read my Bible very well and shall choose for myself."[1] We should never underestimate ordinary Christians' knowledge of the Bible simply because they are not "professional Christians." In an earlier time the Huguenots used to say, "His Bible in his hands, a Protestant is a small pope."[2] Unfortunately, this is probably not so much the case nowadays. But the point is that as a young man, Ted Geisel had plenty of opportunity to get to know his Bible "very well"; and no one can really know the Bible well without at the same time wanting to somehow put this knowledge to good use—even if its power must sometimes be carefully hidden inside artistic booby traps.

It would seem that *The Lorax* is about faith, Christian faith, faith in Christ, faith's short supply in the world, and yet all the world's need for this faith. When Christ said, "If you have faith the size of a mustard seed, you will say to this mountain, 'Move from here to there,' and it will move; and nothing will be impossible for you" (Matt. 17:21), he was not just speaking to the disciples or to me individually, but he was speaking to the whole world. But the world, by its very nature, finds it difficult—even impossible—to believe in Christ, and so it believes instead in something supremely easy to believe in, namely, the world and the things of the world. This is what the story's "once" is all about. Once upon a time, we've been told, the world was like a beautiful garden filled with

> those trees! Those *trees!*
> *Those Truffula trees!*
> All my life I'd been searching
> for trees such as these.

All of us for all of our lives search for beautiful, graceful trees such as these, and originally, once upon a time, they were ours, we *were* those trees ourselves. This is how it all started, as the Once-ler recounts:

> It all started way back . . .
> such a long, long time back.

But then, after this perfectly beautiful "In the beginning," something went terribly, horribly, hideously wrong. For soon people realized that the Truffula trees could be used to supply people with all those things that they think they need—their "Thneeds," in other words. This meant that the Truffula trees would no longer be appreciated for their original purpose. And what was that? They were to represent their designer. Like him they would be "full of grace and truth" (John 1:14)—Tru-fulla trees.

The story of the two types of trees in the garden of Eden is not in the Bible to teach us *how* the situation got to be what it now is, but simply to teach us *what* the situation is. It is said that *once* the situation was wonderful, but however it happened there is now another *once*, another starting point, and *this* starting point from which all of us now originate is absolutely horrible. This is "the old Once-ler" that all of us now start out serving and remain slaves to. The New Testament knows "very well" this starting point of original sin, "the old Once-ler." For example (with my emphasis):

> You who were *once* slaves of sin have become obedient from
> the heart. . . . For just as you *once* yielded your members to
> impurity, . . . so now yield your members to righteousness.
> (Rom. 6:17, 19 RSV)

> you were dead through the trespasses and sins in which you
> *once* walked. . . . Among these we all *once* lived in the pas-
> sions of our flesh.
> (Eph. 2:1–3 RSV)

And you, who *once* were estranged and hostile in mind, doing evil deeds, he has now reconciled in his body of flesh.
(Col. 1:21–22 RSV)

And just as the central human problem in the Bible and in *The Lorax* seems to revolve around this old Once-ler, the answer to this problem seems to hinge on the meaning that both of them can put into "the one word"—as it's printed in *The Lorax*—namely, "UNLESS." It's amazing how many of the most important elements in Dr. Seuss's parable of *The Lorax* are represented in Jesus' parable of "the vine and the branches." Check it out, paying close attention to how Jesus uses "unless" in this passage:

I am the true vine, and my Father is the vinedresser. Every branch in me that bears no fruit he *cuts away*, and every branch that does bear fruit he prunes to make it bear even more. . . . Remain in me, *as I in you*. As a branch cannot bear fruit all by itself, *unless* it remains part of the vine, neither can you *unless* you remain in me. I am the vine, you are the branches. Whoever remains in me, *with me in him*, bears fruit in plenty; for *cut off* from me you can do nothing. Anyone who does not remain in me is thrown away like a branch—and withers; these branches are collected and *thrown on the fire* and are *burnt*.
(John 15:1–2, 4–6 NJB)

Unless the vine and the branches remain together, the branches, like the cut-down Truffula trees in the story, are doomed to only producing "smogulous smoke." Also, the true vine is *in* the branches, just as the Lorax comes "out of the stump of the [Truffulla] tree."

So who then is this "Lorax" on whom so much seems to depend and around whom the entire story centers? And why is the Lorax often referred to, as in the story's first words, as "the *Lifted* Lorax"? "What *was* the Lorax? / And why was it there?" "Lorax" is a word I've never heard anywhere.

Well, it just may be that "Lorax" is an acronym, a word made up from initials and other pieces of words that usually appear in a set phrase—like, for instance, a title Jesus is given in the book of Acts,

"the Lord and Christ" (2:36 NJB)

can become

"the Lor   a   X."

Also in Acts this same Lord and Christ is twice referred to as the "lifted" Lord and Christ (Acts 1:9, 2:33). When Dr. Seuss first introduces us to the Lorax, who is pulling himself "out of the stump of the tree I'd chopped down," this scene is illustrated by an unusually large picture in which the Lorax is surrounded by a colorful border consisting of pointed beams of light, all of which are radiating from— but at the same time pointing at— the Lorax. A kind of Dr. Seuss-type halo, in others words. Dr. Seuss seemed to have a fondness for Isaiah, chapter 11,[3] the first verse of which introduces us to the Messiah and his new age by saying: "A shoot shall come *out from the stump* of Jesse" (Isa. 11:1). When Dr. Seuss told one interviewer about his audiences, "You've got to sneak up on them," I don't think he was kidding.[4]

After the Lorax is lifted "through a hole in the smog," we don't see him anymore, just as we don't see Christ anymore in the New Testament after "he ascended into heaven," to use the Apostles' Creed's words. But at the very end of the story we are told that if we can just use the last of the Truffula Seeds to "Grow a forest" ("And Truffula Trees are what everyone needs")—

Then the Lorax
and all of his friends
may come back.

Or, as Jesus could say about his own "second coming," "when the Son of Man comes, will he find faith on earth?" (Luke

18:8). This, it seems to me, is what *The Lorax* is about. Basically it's asking the same question: Will Christian faith finally survive on earth?

Earlier I quoted something Horatio said to Hamlet. Now I'd like to turn that around and adapt something Hamlet said to Horatio:

> There are more things in Dr. Seuss and Mr. Geisel, Horatio,
> Than are dreamt of in your ordinary children's books.*

Notes

1. Quoted in Percy M. Young, *Handel*, new revised ed. (New York: Collier Books, 1963), 194. See also Paul Henry Lang, *George Frideric Handel* (New York: W. W. Norton & Co., 1966), 342.

2. Quoted in René Huyghe, *Van Gogh* (New York: Crown Publishers, 1958), 26.

3. Note the apparent allusion to Isaiah 11 in chapter 7, "'MY WORD!' God and Horton Faithfully Hatching the Brand New." Also, in Dr. Seuss's 1949 book *Bartholomew and the Oobleck*, there would seem to be a rather obvious reference to Isaiah 11:6: "and a little child shall lead them." At the end of the story, the foolish old king's page boy, Bartholomew (the name of one of the twelve disciples of Jesus), saves the entire kingdom and its king by giving the king some very New Testament–sounding advice: "You ought to be saying some plain *simple* words!" What words? "It *is* all my fault! And I *am* sorry!" the king finally admits. These are the words that immediately save the kingdom. "And then," we are told, "Bartholomew took the old King by the sleeve . . . and *led* him up the steps of the high bell tower. He put the bell rope into His Majesty's royal hands and the King himself rang the holiday bell" (emphasis added).

4. David Dempsey, "The Significance of Dr. Seuss," *New York Times Book Review*, May 11, 1958.

---

*There are more things in Heaven and earth, Horatio, Than are dreamt of in your philosophy (1.5.166).

5

Marvin K. Mooney and Christ's Command to Moonkind

Without Christ, the earth is really more like the moon, a "dead planet" that circles endlessly around a center that it has no awareness of. When we say that someone "moons around," we mean—as the dictionary tells us—that this person "wanders about passing time listlessly or aimlessly." So without Christ, "mankind" is actually more like "moonkind"—that is, a large bunch of "moonies," wandering around aimlessly or listlessly or "spiritlessly," as the dictionary defines *listlessness*.

Without Christ, all life on planet Earth, and planet Earth itself, is ultimately meaningless or moot—or "moont." That is, the planet and life on it may seem to be moving, may seem to be making progress or making some difference or some sense or "going somewhere," but actually this is only an optical illusion. Without Christ, as far as any of us knows the only destination to which anything is finally going is to death or the grave or to nonbeing. Without Christ, we all instinctively know this in our bones, and so we "moon about." No one is really going anywhere. Without Christ, it is as the book of Ecclesiastes saw very clearly long, long ago: "All is vanity":

"Futile, empty and meaningless!" says Ecclesiastes. "Fleeting, incomprehensible and pointless! All things are vanity!" (Eccles. 1:2)[1] Or, as Shakespeare had "damned Macbeth" conclude:

> Life's but . . . a tale
> Told by an idiot, full of sound and fury,
> Signifying nothing.
> (5.5.24, 26–28)

"Life doesn't really mean anything, so to hell with everything," we moonies tend to bitterly think and feel and act.

If there ever has been a good representative of all of us moonies, it's Marvin K. Mooney in Dr. Seuss's book *Marvin K. Mooney—Will You PLEASE GO NOW!* Marvin K. Mooney is definitely not going anywhere but instead is stuck on "dead center." Marvin K. is a "twerp," just like the little twerp we see in Dr. Seuss's *Horton Hears a Who.* That is, he's a small, insignificant looking nerd, wearing something like a jumpsuit with "feet" in it and a large button in front and pockets on either side. This story appears in one of Dr. Seuss's "Bright and Early Books for Beginning Beginners" and therefore it's a study in simplicity—including *spiritual* basics.

When we first meet Marvin K. he's perfectly self-contained —hands in pockets, smugness across a face of indifference, and obviously not interested in listening to anyone. He stands in the middle of a small circular throw rug consisting of three concentric circles. Then from off stage right appears the arm of someone wearing a wristwatch, and the owner of the arm and wristwatch proceeds to point to off left stage and to tell Marvin K.:

> The time has come.
> The time is now.
> Just go. Go. GO!
> I don't care how.

This is followed by the voice making a multitude of colorful and zany suggestions as to *how* Marvin K. Mooney might like to go, all of which are accompanied by the voice's assurance that it doesn't matter how Marvin K. goes, just so he goes and goes and gets going *now*. And of course, all of these suggested modes of going give full freedom to Dr. Seuss's wildly hilarious imagination, both in the showing and the telling.

For instance, Marvin is told that he can go by foot, cow, jet, broomstick, or even in an old blue shoe, as long as he goes, and goes now. Then the voice takes on a much more emphatic tone and, with the hand practically throwing Marvin off the throw rug, says:

> I said GO and GO I meant.

And then in the story's last picture, Marvin happily walks off the rug and waves to the hand, which is now waving back. The story concludes:

> The time had come.
> SO . . .
> Marvin WENT.

That's it! That's Dr. Seuss's *Marvin K. Mooney—Will You PLEASE GO NOW!* It's also very close to Christ's command to all the "Mooneys" of the world. In the New Testament there is a brief passage that is famously known as "the Great Commission." It appears at the very end of Matthew's Gospel and begins with the command to GO! It goes like this:

> Jesus came and said to them, "All authority in heaven and on earth has been given to me. Go therefore and make disciples of all nations, baptizing them in the name of the Father and of the Son and of the Holy Spirit, and teaching them to obey everything that I have commanded you. And remember, I am with you always, to the end of the age."
> (Matt. 28:18–20)

Basically, this is what all followers of Jesus are commanded to do. They are to *go* and make disciples of all nations.

There is another centrally important verse in the New Testament, in which Jesus tells his disciples very clearly what it means to follow him. This is "the new commandment" that Jesus gives his disciples on the night before his arrest and crucifixion. These two commandments are basically saying the same thing, and together the Great Commission and the new commandment do a wonderful job of clarifying and elaborating each other. The "new commandment" tells us:

> I give you a new commandment: love one another; as I have loved you, so you are to love one another.
>
> (John 13:34 REB)

In other words, we are to go and love others as Christ has loved us. And how has Christ loved us? He has made us his disciples. He has brought us into this special relationship with himself, which includes knowledge of him and faith in him. In this particular way the disciples are now to love others. In everything they do, they attempt to share with others the dearest thing they have—their faith in Christ. From the perspective of the Christian faith, this is exactly what it means to love others and to love Christ: to "go and make disciples."

And this commandment/commission is the only thing that can ever get people off their spiritual moons and enable them to be real participants in life. It doesn't just give people something to do—it gives them the only thing to do that is finally and truly satisfying. In anything else, people—all people—will only remain spiritual Mooneys, stuck on dead center, not really having any meaningful direction, not really knowing what it's all about or what they are really for. What are people for? People are for *giving*—that is, giving to others the love of God that is made certain in following Christ. People are *for* "going and making disciples."

They are for going *NOW*. Anything that prevents us from going *NOW* means we're really serving the priority that prevents us from going *NOW*. For instance, "to another [Jesus] said, 'Follow me.' But he said, 'Lord, first let me go and bury

By permission of John Deering and Creators Syndicate, Inc.

my father.' But Jesus said to him, 'Let the dead bury their own dead; but as for you, go and proclaim the kingdom of God" (Luke 9:59–60). Also, *HOW* we go is up to us. One of the great freedoms that Christians have is that they no longer live "under law," as Paul puts it (Rom. 6:14). That is, they are no longer slaves to a bunch of dead, wooden rules and regulations, but they are free to serve the command of their Lord according to their own "lights"—according to their own faithful thinking and intelligence and creativity. Rulebooks and regulations can be very helpful at times, but "the law" is no longer our Lord. Not the dead law, but only the living Lord is the Christian's ultimate guide.

So, then, this is the command that came to Marvin K. Mooney, and it's Christ's command for all of the rest of us Mooneys as well:

The time has come.
The time is now.
Just go. Go. GO!
I don't care how.

As soon as we obey this command we are off dead center and on our way. If we don't obey it, we are still just "spinning our wheels" and "mooning around."

Oh, the spiritual juice
That's on the loose
In Dr. Seuss!

Notes

1. Robert Short, *A Time to Be Born—A Time to Die: The Images and Insights of "Ecclesiastes" for Today* (New York: Harper & Row, 1973), 7.

6

For All Those Who Have Had Trouble Getting to Solla Sollew

I think this is probably my favorite Dr. Seuss story—*I Had Trouble in Getting to Solla Sollew*—because I've had trouble getting there too! The story may not be autobiographical as far as Ted Geisel was concerned, but it's sure biographical as far as I'm concerned. It's a story about me. Maybe it's about you too.

And this is because it's always a troubling trail that leads to the truth. The path to wisdom is always a downward one. But we'd rather this not be the case. Like Lucy in *Peanuts*, we'd rather not face a life with ups and downs; we'd rather life consist only of "ups and ups and ups." So as soon as we bump into hardships, we set out for the land of nothing but softships. As soon as we trip over troubles, we set "off to the City of Solla Sollew . . . where they *never* have troubles! At least, very few." In Dr. Seuss's story of Solla Sollew, our hero "never had ever had troubles before." Never, that is, until one day he stubs his toe on a rock, and "SOCK! What a shock!"

In eternity's scheme of things, this isn't unusual. The call from God is always a wakeup call, a startling shock. This is the way it has to start, especially when you consider that most of us arrive on the scene much like our hero—young, happy, and carefree. When one lives this kind of soft, dreamy existence, then a sure 'nuf socking, shocking wakeup call is definitely called for. But what we wake up to in this situation is the awareness that life is *filled* with trouble:

> There I was,
> All completely surrounded by trouble.

And so our young hero quite understandably, and just like practically all the rest of us, takes off for "Solla Sollew . . . Where they *never* have troubles! At least very few." We all tend to look for this magic city of no-troubles—this Utopia, this El Dorado, this Elysium. "Oh, give me a home where the buffalo roam . . . where seldom is heard a discouraging word." "I left my heart in San Francisco." "Why, oh, why did I ever leave Wyoming?" "Oh, I wish I were in Dixie, away! away!" "California, here I come!" And just like we look for utopian places, we also hanker for utopian forms of government, utopian relationships, utopian jobs—Solla Sollew, in other words, "Where they *never* have troubles! At least very few."

I have no idea how Dr. Seuss came up with this colorful Seussism, "Solla Sollew." But for me, "Solla" suggests *sola*, the Latin word for "solely" or "alone." "Sollew" might be a Seussinated form of celestial or "sollewstial"—"heavenly," in other words. So does "Solla Sollew" mean "solely heavenly"? Heavens! I don't know. It might just mean "Solla Sollew," a place "where they *never* have troubles! At least, very few."

Anyway, our little Everyperson then sets off for Solla Sollew, only to learn that looking for the troublesless can itself be very troublesome. Originally, "Not anything ever went wrong." Now everything goes wrong. He manages to catch a ride with a character who's headed for the same destination, but the road is so "tricky" it makes his "stomach feel icky." Even the camel, which pulls the two travelers over the rocks and through the night on a "One-Wheeler Wubble," itself gets sick. But no camel doctor is to be found, and soon our hero is himself pulling both camel and friend up mountains. "Teamwork" is what his lazy friend calls all of our young pilgrim's trouble-filled efforts. Soon our hero deposits friend and camel at a camel doctor's office, and there he's assured:

> Your troubles are practically all at an end.
> Just run down that hill and around the next bend.

But around the next bend he runs into the worst storm in all literature since *King Lear*. It's "the Midwinter Jicker" that

> came early this year
> And it's not going to be very comfy 'round here.

And it isn't. Instead, our hero is now sent crashing and thrashing in an epic flood, provoking the same age-old question expressed by humankind at least since the time of Job:

> "Now I really don't see
> Why troubles like this have to happen to *me!*"

After floating for days he grabs hold of a rope, only to find that on the other end of the rope is General Genghis Khan Schmitz, whose rope should remind us that when we're at the end of our ropes we can really be dopes; we'll often frantically grab hold of anything—like mystery, miracle, authority—you name it. We can make a false savior out of anything when we're desperate enough! The General quickly drafts our little trouble-avoider into a war that Schmitz is fighting and losing, a war being fought for no discernible reason. Then, after being betrayed by Schmitz, he dives into a vent and through a dark tunnel, a tunnel with a strong undertow of biblical overtones:

> Troubles! I wished
> I had never been born!

—echoing Job when he "cursed the day of his birth" (3:1) and tells us "I have no rest; but trouble comes" (3:26).

"I was down there three days," our traveling trouble treader tells us, just like Jesus tells of Jonah in the belly of the whale and the Son of man in the heart of the earth "for three days" (Matt. 12:40). What is this, a baptism or a crucifixion? But when we consider that baptism is only a symbol for crucifixion in the first place (Rom. 6:3–4), then we can see that this "frightful black tunnel" will do very nicely for hinting at both.

Anyway, immediately following our little friend's escape from the tunnel through a tiny trap door, he finally and actually makes it to the doorway of Solla Sollew, but there's just one problem—the one key to Solla Sollew's door no longer works. So the doorkeeper suggests that he and his new friend take off for a neighboring city, Boola Boo Ball, whose townsfolk have no troubles at all.

And here our story comes to an abrupt end: the little guy decides against making the trip to Boola Boo Ball but instead starts back toward home, saying

> I know I'll have troubles.
> I'll, maybe, get stung.
> I'll always have troubles.
> I'll, maybe, get bit . . .
> . . . .
> But I've bought a big bat.
> I'm all ready, you see.
> Now my troubles are going
> To have troubles with *me!*

Those who have commented on this story usually tell us it teaches us that we shouldn't run away from our troubles but that we should stay and face them. And that's it?!? In logic or law this is called "begging the question." For the question is not so much whether we should run from trouble or stay; but the question is precisely *how* to face trouble so there'll be no need to run away. And it seems to me that this wonderful story has at least three strong suggestions to make about how to face troubles so that

Without further fear or fuss
Our troubles will have troubles with *us!* (Dr. Short)

First, Christian faith, like the rest of the world generally, is aware of the benefits that can come from trouble—from suffering, from discipline and hard work, and from problem solving. All this the world well knows and Christian faith with it. We all know that good judgment comes from experience and experience comes from bad judgment. The difference is that Christian faith has an *infinitely greater* appreciation of trouble than the world does. This is because faith realizes that trouble, or suffering, is the doorway through which it has come to learn of its wonderful new Lord and that, furthermore, trouble, suffering, is also necessary for keeping faith strong. Faith will always be strongest when the believer is weakest. Strong people don't need faith like weak people do. This is why Paul could write:

> Three times I prayed the Lord to relieve me of [a thorn in the flesh], but he told me, "It is enough for you to have my grace: it is in weakness that my power is fully felt." So I am proud to boast of all my weakness, and thus to have the power of Christ resting on my life. It makes me content, for Christ's sake, with weakness, insults, trouble, persecution, and calamity; for I am strong just when I am weak.
>
> (2 Cor. 12:7–10 Moffatt)

In this way trouble is one of God's greatest gifts to us. I used to have a dog named Trouble. People often asked how I chose that name. It's from *Macbeth*, I would say, always glad that they had given me the opportunity to quote a great line: "The love that follows us sometime is our trouble, / Which still we thank as love" (Macbeth 1.6.11). "*Affliction* is a *treasure*," John Donne wrote, "and scarce any man hath *enough* of it. No man hath *affliction* enough that is not matured and ripened by it, and made fit for *God* by that *affliction*."[1]

Furthermore, trouble can help us to be grateful that we are living, breathing human beings and not rocks or corpses with no trouble. There is a marvelous scene in *Zorba the Greek* that illustrates this perfectly. Zorba's spineless young friend, "the boss," is having trouble getting to Solla Sollew—that is, meeting a beautiful young woman he's seen. He tells Zorba:

> "I don't want any trouble! . . .
> "You don't want any trouble!" Zorba exclaimed in stupefaction. "And pray, what do you want, then?"
> I did not answer.
> "Life is trouble," Zorba continued. "Death, no. To live—do you know what that means? To undo your belt and look for trouble!"[2]

The second suggestion is that Christians are better able to face troubles because they know that troubles are not forever and that furthermore their solutions don't have to be ultimately meaningless. "No wonder we do not lose heart!" Paul says. "Our troubles are slight and short-lived; and their outcome an eternal glory which outweighs them far" (2 Cor. 4:16–17 NEB). But if there is no "eternal glory," and therefore no God in whose service we do battle against trouble, then all of our "successes" in combating trouble are ultimately meaningless; all "success" is finally defeated by death. So in this case, why even bother resisting trouble? On the other hand, Christians, with their God of "eternal glory," "know that in the Lord your labor cannot be lost" (1 Cor. 15:58 NEB). And so the faith of Christians gives them a hope and a courage that the world doesn't know, a hope and a courage that no trouble—not even death—can finally discourage or disappoint or defeat. As Paul describes the source of this courage:

> We triumph even in our troubles, knowing that trouble produces endurance, endurance produces character, and character produces hope—*a hope which never disappoints us.*
> (Rom. 5:3–5 Moffatt)

And this courage in turn makes Christians unafraid of getting in trouble or even *making* trouble in the service of their Lord. This attitude toward trouble also makes them carefree and happy even in the *midst* of trouble. As F. R. Maltby has pointed out:

> Jesus promised his disciples three things—
> that they would be completely fearless,
> absurdly happy, and in constant trouble.[3]

No doubt this is why Dr. Seuss's disciples also know plenty of trouble and also get banged around by it quite a bit.

© Grimmy, Inc. King Features Syndicate

Dr. Seuss's story has one more powerful thing to suggest about overcoming trouble. (Oh, the power of suggestion!) And in this third thing we really do knock trouble over the head.

We know that Dr. Seuss was at least on speaking terms with the Bible's 23rd Psalm. We know this because Judith and Neil Morgan's excellent biography of Dr. Seuss (and Mr. Geisel) tells us that early in his career the fun-loving Ted Geisel, along with a friend who shared his "love of language and . . . dislike of pomposity," dreamed of launching a private detective agency. They wanted to call their firm, "Surely, Goodness and Mercy." And their slogan, from the same source, would be: "Will follow you all the days of your life" (Ps. 23:6).[4] Surely it was goodness and mercy that prevented Dr. Seuss and his friend from following up on this idea.

But the point is that Dr. Seuss, knowing Psalm 23 as he must have—with its "enemies," its "valley of the shadow," its downward progression along a perilous footpath—also knew the part about "thy rod and thy staff, they comfort me." For this is the way, in a manner of speaking, that *I Had Trouble in Getting to Solla Sollew* is concluded, with the little guy and his "big bat," ready to face his troubles. And indeed in the story's final picture we do see this big bat and the confident look on our hero's face as he wields it, heading straight toward combat with his troubles. "I'm all ready, you see." Sure looks and sounds like Paul to me! Check it out:

> I have learned to be content, whatever the circumstances may be. I know how to live when things are difficult and I know how to live when things are prosperous. In general and in particular I have learned the secret of facing either plenty or poverty. *I am ready for anything* through the strength of the one who lives within me.
>
> (Phil. 4:11–13 Phillips; emphasis added)

He is all ready because of that bat, that "rod and staff" of Psalm 23. Can that rod and staff, that bat, be seen as Christ, "the one who lives within me"? Bat of course! The New Testament writers saw Christ prefigured all through the Old Testament. Luther is a typical New Testament interpreter of this verse, seeing this bat, this rod and staff, this Christ, as the world's number one trouble-bopper:

> "Thy rod and Thy staff, they comfort me." It is as though [the psalmist] would say: "In all my anxieties and troubles I

find nothing on earth that might help to satisfy me. But then God's Word is my rod and my staff. . . . [The Lord] not only strengthens and comforts me with this same Word in all distresses and temptations, but . . . also redeems me from all my enemies."[5]

When we have trouble in getting to Solla Sollew, it's good to remember that we are always called to go to bat for our Lord. This is why the psalmist reminds us that

God is our refuge and strength, a very present help in trouble.
(Ps. 46:1 RSV)

One thing more: just what "trouble" are we talking about here? Finally we're talking about trouble in its most all-inclusive sense—yours, mine, everyone's; now and forever; sin, evil, guilt, suffering, injustice, death and taxes—everything we call "trouble." Is there anyone or anything that will finally overcome and defeat all trouble? Oh, yes! Our Lord has already done it! Ultimately—and this is known only through obedience to Christ alone—God himself will get us all to Solla Sollew, to the "solely heavenly." And so Jesus can say,

In the world you will have trouble. But courage! The victory is mine; I have conquered the world.
(John 16:33 NEB)

So then, until this final victory completely takes over, batter up!

Notes

1. "Devotions upon Emergent Occasions," *The Complete Poetry and Selected Prose of John Donne,* ed. Charles M. Coffin (New York: Modern Library, 1952), 441.

2. Nikos Kazantzakis, *Zorba the Greek,* trans. Carl Wildman (New York: Ballantine, 1952), 115–16.

3. Quoted in William Barclay, *The Gospel of Luke*, rev. ed. (Philadelphia: Westminster Press, 1975), 77.

4. Judith and Neil Morgan, *Dr. Seuss and Mr. Geisel: A Biography* (New York: Random House, 1995), 73.

5. *Luther's Works*, vol. 12, *Selected Psalms 1*, ed. Jaroslav Pelikan (St. Louis: Concordia Publishing House, 1955), 169.

7

"MY WORD!" God and Horton Faithfully Hatching the Brand New

There are so many surprising connecting points between Christian faith and Dr. Seuss's stories, that we often wonder if the good Doctor didn't know what he was doing. Of course he knew exactly what he was doing when it came to writing and illustrating his marvelously charming stories for both young people and adults. But did he know something more? Did Dr. Seuss, like so many great writers and artists, purposely hide truth "within the center," to use Shakespeare's way of putting it? (*Hamlet* 2.2.157–59). Shakespeare himself did this. So if Shakespeare could deftly sneak truth into the center of his creations and not tell a soul, why couldn't Dr. Seuss do the same thing? In the meantime, Dr. Seuss still, willy-nilly, provides us with many great "parables for the kingdom of God" (Mark 4:30).

Horton Hatches the Egg is the story of a lovable, huge-hearted elephant, Horton, who is talked into sitting in a tree on lazy Mayzie bird's little egg while she leaves her nest and flies off for a vacation. Horton realizes he's hardly cut out for the job but feels sorry for Mayzie, and so agrees to do it anyway:

"You want a vacation. Go fly off and take it.
I'll sit on your egg and I'll try not to break it.
I'll stay and be faithful. I mean what I say."
"Toodle-oo!" sang out Mayzie and fluttered away.

But this is just the beginning of Horton's troubles, because Mayzie is soon having such a good time in Palm Beach that she's "Decided she'd NEVER go back to her nest!" Nevertheless, "An elephant's faithful / One hundred percent," as Horton keeps telling us. And so he keeps faith with Mayzie and remains the constant egg-sitter even while the seasons roll by—including elephant-sized storms and blizzards.

Then three hunters with rifles show up in Horton's jungle and decide that instead of shooting Horton they'll capture him and sell him, tree and all, to a circus.

The "terribly funny" spectacle of a live "elephant sitting on
    top of a tree"
Will bring in far more money than a poor ol' dead Hor-
    ton, you see. (Dr. Short)

Then, still in the tree and on Mayzie's egg after a horrible over-land-and-sea trip to New York, Horton is sold to a circus that takes him all over the United States. Finally, one day lazy Mayzie flies by and recognizes Horton at exactly the time her egg begins to hatch. Of course, Mayzie now wants the egg back. But before she can reclaim it, out hatches a little elephant-bird with ears and a tail and a trunk just like Horton's— but also with wings and a big smile and a readiness to fly. And because all the delighted people had not seen anything like this before, they then send Horton and his little Elephant-Bird "home Happy, one hundred per cent!" A happy Horton ending if there ever was one.

To say that *Horton Hatches the Egg* is a retelling of the New Testament's Christmas story may sound like a bit of a stretch, but the fact is that this story can easily be seen this way. The New Testament's story (and this is why it's called the NEW Testament) tells us about something brand new in human history—the birth of "the God-man," as great an incongruity as it's possible to imagine.

The Horton story tells us about a similar incongruity that is likewise "brand new"— the birth of the ELEPHANT-BIRD:

> Then they cheered and they *cheered* and CHEERED more
>   and more.
> *They'd never seen anything like it before!*
> "My goodness! *My gracious!*" they shouted.
>   "MY WORD!
> *It's something brand new!* IT'S AN ELEPHANT-BIRD!!"

"In the beginning was the Word, . . . and the Word was God. . . . And the Word became flesh and lived among us" (John 1:1, 14) is the basic meaning of the Christian teaching of the incarnation—the doctrine of the God-man. God became a particular, historical, flesh and blood, brand new, and unique man—Jesus. The Lord was born! And where and how did this infinite metamorphosis first appear? In a stall for animals with a lot of people standing around staring "with their eyes popping out!" to use Dr. Seuss's words. At the beginning of this event, according to the New Testament, an angel appears who bids the people to be of good cheer and to "be not afraid; for behold I bring you good news of a great joy which will come to all the people; for to you is born this day a Savior, who is Christ the Lord" (Luke 2:10–11 RSV). Or, to go back to Dr. Seuss's way of describing this story, the people . . .

> . . . cheered and they *cheered* and they CHEERED more
>   and more.
> *They'd never seen anything like it before!* "My goodness! *My
>   gracious!*" they shouted. "MY WORD!
> *It's something brand new!* IT'S AN ELEPHANT-BIRD!!"

These are two ways of telling the Christmas story. But is there one, single word in all of *Horton Hatches the Egg* that even suggests that it was Christmas that Dr. Seuss had in mind in this story? Nope. Hardly a word. There is, however, one interesting little tidbit. In a detail tucked away inconspicuously in the story, Dr. Seuss tells us that when the egg finally hatched

> There rang out the noisiest ear-splitting squeaks
> From the egg that he'd sat on for fifty-one weeks!

Why fifty-one weeks? Why not fifty-three or forty-five or any other number of weeks?

> Well, when does Christmas occur every year?
> Why, just after the fifty-first week of the year, my dear!
> (Dr. Short)

"Fifty-one weeks!" Then Christmas—the celebration of the birth of the GOD-MAN!

> Or, if it is preferred,
> The birth of the ELEPHANT-BIRD. (Dr. Short)

One other point to consider: Where is the Elephant-Bird born? Up in a tree and out on a limb. But wasn't the God-Man born "in a manger" or animal stall? Yes, but it has often been said that Christ's crucifixion began at his birth. After all, the delivery room where Christ was born wasn't exactly a bed of roses. So the similarity between these two births still holds. But what is the significance of this tree or crucifixion in both stories? Of course it's impossible to exhaust the meaning of Christ's cross. But what would seem to be the meaning of this tree or cross as Dr. Seuss points to it and to its meaning for us today? . . . its meaning for us in this story, *Horton Hatches the Egg*?

In the Christian view of things, the doorway through which we come to know God is his "Word made flesh," this utterly brand new creature he has hatched for us. Making this discovery, we ourselves become new creatures and we cheer and we *cheer* and we CHEER more and more. For "if any one is in Christ, he is a new creature" (2 Cor. 5:17 RSV). But the doorway through which this Word is made real to us is a tree, a cross, a crucifixion—and not just the tree of someone else, but also a tree that we ourselves have known and participated in. For logically how can anyone really get excited about the birth of the Elephant-Bird and cheer and *cheer* and CHEER, unless they themselves have known something of this tree's sobering sorrow. And of course this purifying suffering of our own is what God's "Elephant-Bird" was talking about when

> to everybody he said, "Anyone who wants to be a follower of mine must renounce self; day after day he must take up his cross, and follow me. Whoever wants to save his life will lose it, but whoever loses his life for my sake will save it."
> (Luke 9:23–24 REB)

In this way the tree, which began in the story as a horrible curse, finally becomes for us a life-giving blessing, providing a totally "new birth" (John 3:7) of our own. And so I submit that

> All of this "brand new" as it turns out
> Is what *Horton Hatches the Egg* is about! (Dr. Short)

But there's one more page, the final scene, of this story that's not to be overlooked. Dr. Seuss illustrates this scene by having Horton happily carrying his equally happy little Elephant-Bird back into the jungle filled with animals, all delighted to see Horton and his Elephant-Bird. And so the story ends by saying:

> And they sent him home
> Happy,
> One hundred per cent!

With this great variety of animals on hand to greet Horton and his Elephant-Bird (including a very large lion in the foreground on the right), it's easy to be reminded of artist Edward Hicks's *Peaceable Kingdom* paintings in which we also see a great jumble of animals—including humans—not ordinarily on speaking terms. And this variety is meant to say to us that eventually we'll

Art Resource, NY

all get along; eventually everything will be alright—*everything*
and *everyone*. The Old Testament paints this scene this way—
the very scene Hicks had in mind:

> Righteousness shall be the belt around his waist,
>   and faithfulness the belt around his loins.
> The wolf shall live with the lamb,
>   the leopard shall lie down with the kid,
> the calf and the lion and the fatling together,
>   and a little child shall lead them.
> The cow and the bear shall graze,
>   their young shall lie down together;
>   and the lion shall eat straw like the ox.
> The nursing child shall play over the hole of the asp.
>   and the weaned child shall put its hand on the adder's
>   den.
> They will not hurt or destroy
>   on all my holy mountain;

for the earth will be full of the knowledge of the LORD
as the waters cover the sea. (Isa, 11:5–9)

In the New Testament this vision of the end of history is the
same:

> For in Christ the complete being of God, by God's own
> choice, came to dwell. Through him God chose to reconcile
> the whole universe to himself, making peace through the
> shedding of his blood upon the cross—to reconcile all
> things, whether on earth or in heaven, through him alone.
> (Col. 1:19–20 NEB)

Of course, all of these pictures—those from Dr. Seuss, Hicks,
the Old Testament, and the New Testament—are just the
opposite of the pictures we have seen of sinners being cast into
an "eternal hell." Thank goodness Dr. Seuss's good news really
is *good* news and not some ridiculous and terrifying travesty of
it. For the truly good news is that we know through Christ that
ultimately *all* will get "home happy, one hundred percent!"

8

How Christmas Stole the Grinch's Heart

Readers Digest once described Dr. Seuss as "the most popular children's author and illustrator in history."[1] We can always tell when something's popular. Cartoonists start commenting on it:

© United Feature Syndicate, Inc.

More recently, I found the following conversation in *Geech*:

© Jerry Bittle/dist. by United Feature Syndiicate, Inc.

One of the reasons Dr. Seuss (or Theodor Seuss Geisel) has become so popular is that his simplicity not only hits it off with kids, but his stories also carry a kind of "profundity-in-simplicity" quality that enables grownups to appreciate them too. His stories are a bit like the parables of Jesus, then, in that their simplicity is deceptive. Charming, childlike little tales suddenly become meaningful in deeply life-changing ways. They sneak up on us. They become Trojan horses or sugar-coated medicine. They are the wise cat in the otherwise empty hat. For this reason Dr. Seuss's stories are good examples of the modern, updated parables that are always needed by the church if the church is to speak effectively to its time. Luther was talking about the church's need for new parables better suited to a new time when he wrote:

> We see that . . . young people are easily moved by fables and tales and are also led with pleasure and love to art and wisdom; which pleasure and love become the greater if an Aesop or similar masked or carnival figure is presented, who expresses or produces such art that they pay more heed thereto, and receive and retain the same with laughter.
>
> But not the children only, but one can beguile also the great princes and lords in no better way to wisdom and its use, than that one have fools speak the truth to them. They can tolerate and listen to them, when they will not or cannot tolerate the truth from any wise person; in fact all the world hates the truth if it fits them.
>
> For this reason such wise and great people have fabricated fables, and have one animal speak with another, as if they would say: Now then! No one will listen to the truth, nor tolerate it, and yet we cannot get on without the truth; so we will deck it out, and dress it in gay, false colors, and delightful fables; and though no one will listen to it from a human mouth, yet they will hear it from the mouths of beasts and animals.
>
> —Martin Luther, 1530[2]

Now Dr. Seuss may not at all have intended for his stories to act as present-day parables that could be used by the church, but that doesn't matter. All sorts of things can be seen as "parables of the kingdom," regardless of whatever intention—or no intention at all—might lie behind them. Truth is where you find it. For example, I'll bet the "good Samaritan" or the "prodigal son" never dreamed that their experiences would turn out to be helpful to anyone else. And, as we know, authors and other artists are often influenced by Christ in very deep ways that they themselves can be totally unaware of. The influence of Christ has saturated our culture so widely and deeply that it tends to be built into our ways of thinking and seeing even when we're least conscious of it. By definition, Christian truth in one way or another points to Christ as the way, the truth, and the life, or it's not Christian truth. But when anything does this—either intentionally or unintentionally, either consciously or unconsciously —then this can be seen as "Christian truth." And so if it's possible, as Shakespeare can say in *As You Like It*, to find

> tongues in trees, books in the running brooks,
> Sermons in stones, and good in everything,

then why not

> Christian truths
> In Dr. Seuss? (Dr. Short)

Among Dr. Seuss's stories, *How the Grinch Stole Christmas* is no doubt one of his biggest hits. And one of the reasons for the Grinch's ability to steal our hearts is that it has become a traditional network TV show, showing up every year during the Christmas season. Red, in Brian Basset's *Red and Rover*, gives us a good idea of how the TV Grinch has made this story a popular culture cinch. Red complains to Rover that the Grinch continually gets away with stealing Christmas and says "If you ask me, prison rehabilitation is *not* working on *that* boy."

So it would seem Dr. Seuss knows how to catch our attention. Let's see if he can also help catch our consciences. In which case, to use words from *Hamlet*, "Dr. Seuss is the thing wherein we'll catch consciences for the King!"

How this story is related to the New Testament is really very simple. For we know from the story that the Grinch only *tried* to steal Christmas but was a total flop at the project. And if we're familiar enough with the language of the New Testament, we know that Jesus also talked about those who would attempt to steal (or "rob") his spirit, or joy, from his followers. Jesus said it couldn't be done. Jesus said, "You will be joyful, and no one shall rob you of your joy" (John 16:22 REB). No one will be able to take that joy from you or steal it from you.

The Spirit of Christ, which is really the spirit of Christmas, is unstealable—as the Grinch found out. Try as he did by stealing all the wrappings and trappings of Christmas, the Grinch didn't even come close to stealing the true *spirit* of Christmas. Because the spirit of Christmas isn't dependent on circumstances for its staying power. It goes much deeper and is much stronger than any of the circumstances of this world. So Christmas, the Grinch learned

> "came without ribbons! It came without tags!
> It came without packages, boxes or bags!"
> And he puzzled three hours, till his puzzler was sore.
> *Then* the Grinch thought of something he hadn't before!
> "Maybe Christmas," he thought, "*doesn't* come from a
>   store."
> "Maybe Christmas . . . perhaps . . . means a little bit more!"

Poor Grinch! He didn't realize what he was up against! But he soon found out. And because he found out, he then made a very wise decision: If you can't beat 'em, join 'em!

And this strategy, the strategy behind "If you can't beat 'em, join 'em," is one of the chief strategies that Christians are taught to use. Christ has given us his own Spirit, his joy, his peace. Nothing else in the world can give us this Spirit, and nothing in this world can take it from us—or "steal" it:

> Peace is my parting gift to you, my own peace, such as the
> world cannot give.
>
>   (John 14:27 REB)

Well, we're to let the world see this gift, this peace, which no one can steal or no circumstances of the world can take from us. And the reason we want the world to see it is not so people will think more highly of us, but because they will want it too—they will want something that they know they don't have and that they can see quite clearly that we do have. "If you can't beat 'em, join 'em!" they'll say. They'll join up. They'll join us in joyfully following Christ. They'll quit following things that don't make them happy, and they'll start following something that does make people happy—faith in Jesus as Lord.

The New Testament is full of this kind of advice for Christians: Let the rest of the world see this joy that Christ has given you, that can't be taken from you, and when they can't beat you, they'll join you. For example, just listen to the following three New Testament voices: First, Jesus:

> Nor do men light a lamp and put it under a bushel, but on a stand, and it gives light to all in the house. Let your light so shine before men, that they may see your good works and give glory to your Father who is in heaven.
>
> (Matt. 5:15–16 RSV)

Then Paul says:

> Do everything without grumbling or argument. Show yourselves innocent and above reproach, faultless children of God in a crooked and depraved generation, in which you shine like stars in a dark world and proffer the word of life.
>
> (Phil. 2:14–16 REB)

And finally these words from Peter:

> Your conduct among the surrounding peoples . . . should always be good and right, so that although they may in the usual way slander you as evildoers, yet when disasters come they may glorify God when they see how well you conduct yourselves.
>
> (1 Pet. 2:12 Phillips)

When they see that they can't beat us, they'll join us—just like the Grinch joined the *Whos* when he saw that he obviously couldn't beat them:

> He HADN'T stopped Christmas from coming!
> IT CAME!
> . . . .
> Well . . . in *Who*-ville they say
> That the Grinch's small heart
> Grew three sizes that day!
> . . . .
> And he brought back the toys! And the food for the feast!
> . . . And he . . .
> . . . HE HIMSELF . . . !
> *The Grinch carved the roast beast!*

And this is exactly how one joins up and becomes a follower: one becomes a giver instead of a taker. You not only return the roast beast instead of stealing it, but then you proceed to carve the roast beast and serve it to the others yourself. One becomes a fellow follower only by obeying the same Lord the others obey. It's only obedience to only this Lord that can change us from takers to givers, for it's only in obedience to only this Lord that we are given the experience and power of his love, a love that no one can then steal from us. This is why

> We should keep in mind the words of the Lord Jesus, who himself said, "Happiness lies more in giving than in receiving."
>
> (Acts 20:35 REB)

And when we become fellow followers with the *Whos,* we not only carve the roast beast and serve it ourselves, but then we ourselves also sit down with our fellow followers and enjoy the same meal they enjoy. Now we need our fellow followers not only so they can give to us but also so we can give to them. We need our Lord Jesus not only so he can give to us but also so we can give ourselves to him. For "happiness lies more in giving than in receiving." Therefore "HE HIMSELF . . . ! *The Grinch carved the roast beast!*"

WHO'S THE *WHOS*?

So who's the *Whos*—our fellow followers? Dr. Seuss depicts them in exactly the same way the Bible depicts Christians. For according to the Bible, exactly who is it that the Lord prefers and is always closest to?

> I dwell . . . with him *who* is broken and humble in spirit. . . .
> The one for *whom* I have regard is oppressed and afflicted,
> one *who* reveres my word.
> (Isa. 57:15; 66:2 REB; emphasis added)

That's who!

The *Whos* in *How the Grinch Stole Christmas* are exactly the same kind of *Whos* we find in another Dr. Seuss "who" story— *Horton Hears a Who*. They are the little people, the humble, the weak ones whose weakness leaves plenty of room for God. They are the ones whose huge influence hardly matches the smallness of their size. The *Whos* certainly sound like Christians to me:

> Every *Who* down in *Who*-ville, the tall and the small,
> Was singing! Without any presents at all!

Or as Paul says:

> Rejoice always, pray constantly, give thanks in all circumstances; for this is the will of God in Christ Jesus for you.
> (1 Thess. 5:16–18 RSV)

The *Whos* then are the "faultless children of God in a crooked and depraved generation, in which [they] shine like stars in a dark world" (Phil. 2:14–16 REB).

WHERE DOES ALL OF THIS COME FROM?

"Maybe Christmas," he thought, "*doesn't* come from a
    store.
Maybe Christmas . . . perhaps . . . means a little bit more!"

Because *The Grinch* is a Christmas story, practically everything is said in it—just like everything is said in Christ: "All
things are held together in (Christ)" (Col. 1:17 REB). We learn
from the story who the *Whos* are, what strategy they use in
dealing with others, about their joy that can't be taken from
them, and so forth. But also

> we need to pay attention to
> just what makes the *Whos Whos*. (Dr. Short)

What gives them their unconquerable love and optimism?
The simple answer is—Christmas. Christmas means the coming of God in Christ to us men and women. And his coming
means, first, the message of the unconquerable love of God
given to all of us. It goes to any lengths, overcomes all barriers,
stops at nothing to finally bring all of us—"all the people"—
into the kingdom of this love. Then, second, it gives us the way
whereby we can be sure of this love—and know this message is
true—that is, by following the Christ, "the way," by actively
believing and obeying and trusting in him. Together these two
components are known as "the gospel." They are the good news.
They are the good news that Christmas announces to us: "Be
not afraid; for behold, I bring you good news of great joy which
will come to all the people; for to you is born this day . . . a Savior, who is Christ the Lord" (Luke 2:10–11 RSV). This is where
Christmas comes from, and it is precisely what makes the *Whos
Whos*: it is *who* Christ is and what he has promised to "all the
people." No wonder the *Whos'* love is indeflectable; it comes
from the ultimately indeflectable love of God revealed in
Christmas.

So what is the "moral" of Dr. Seuss's story—its moral for all of us *Whos* and all of us Grinches? Seems to me it is simply this: If God's grace enables us to hang on to Christ and to follow only him as our Lord, then no one will ever be able to steal the real Christmas from us; "[we] will be joyful, and no one shall rob us of [our] joy." Furthermore, if we get good enough at doing this, then

> Not only will unstealable joy belong to us *Whos,*
> But even a few Grinches may come around too!
> (Dr. Short)

Notes

1. James Stewart-Gordon, "Dr. Seuss: Fanciful Sage of Childhood," in *Reader's Digest*, April 1972, 141.
2. From "Luther's Preface to Aesop's Fables," quoted in *Early Protestant Educators*, ed. Frederick Eby (New York: McGraw-Hill, 1931), 153–54.

9

The Good News for You
Through
Horton Hears a Who!

But you, my children, are of God's family, and you have the mastery over these false prophets, because he who inspires you is greater than he who inspires the godless world. They are of that world, and so therefore is their teaching; that is why the world listens to them. But we belong to God, and a man who knows God listens to us, while he who does not belong to God refuses us a hearing. That is how we distinguish the spirit of truth from the spirit of error.

Dear friends, let us love one another, because love is from God. Everyone who loves is a child of God and knows God, but the unloving know nothing of God. For God is love; and his love was disclosed to us in this, that he sent his only Son into the world to bring us life. The love I speak of is not our love for God, but the love he showed to us in sending his Son as the remedy for the defilement of our sins. If God thus loved us, dear friends, we in turn are bound to love one another. Though God has never been seen by any man, God himself dwells in us if we love one another; his love is brought to perfection within us.

Here is the proof that we dwell in him and he dwells in us: he has imparted his Spirit to us. Moreover, we have seen for ourselves, and we attest, that the Father sent the Son to be the saviour of the world, and if a man acknowledges that Jesus is the Son of God, God dwells in him and he dwells in God. Thus we have come to know and believe the love which God has for us.

God is love; he who dwells in love is dwelling in God, and God in him.

1 John 4:4–16 NEB

Did you know that in the parables of Jesus, Jesus would frequently use already existing stories for his own purposes? True. This is why German New Testament scholar Joachim Jeremias can tell us:

Occasional folk-story themes found their way into the parables. We . . . repeatedly find that Jesus himself made use of
such themes.[1]

Whatever their original intent may have been, that didn't stop
Jesus from using these ready-made stories to help him get
across his own teachings. And so it is that I'm now using Dr.
Seuss's *Horton Hears a Who* in the same way. No one can really
know for sure what Dr. Seuss/Mr. Geisel had in mind when he
dreamed up this beautiful little tale. We can't say that Dr. Seuss
couldn't have been thinking in terms of the New Testament
when he created Horton. There are some things in Horton that
are so close to the gospel of Jesus that it makes us wonder if
Horton wasn't secretly designed from the beginning to be "hor-
tatory" in the Christian sense.

> But since we can't really know,
> We'll let this question go. (Dr. Short)

Horton Hears a Who is the story of a lovable elephant, Horton, who has keen ears and a big heart. One day his ears enable
him to hear something none of the other jungle animals can
hear—or see. It's the tiny, frightened voice of the Mayor of
Who-ville, who is shaking with fear because he's afraid his
entire microscopic town—located on just a "speck" floating
past in the breeze—is going to end up in the pool of water
Horton is splashing around in. Convinced that his ears know
what they're hearing, Horton's big heart then takes over; he
gently places the speck "on a very soft clover," and he becomes
determined to protect this whole world of the *Whos,* Mayor
and all. "Because," as Horton says,

> A person's a person, no matter how small.

Uh, oh. For soon all of the other jungle animals are enraged
by one of their number who goes around speaking to a mere
speck. So they decide to chase Horton off and to do away completely with his speck. But Horton is not going to let this hap-

pen and therefore he hopes to get all of the *Whos* in *Who*-ville to make enough noise so that even the kangaroos and the Wickersham family of monkeys can hear the "mad hullabaloo" of the *Whos*. Finally this plan works when, at the last minute, the Mayor discovers one "very small shirker" who hasn't added his voice to the desperate din. And so then it's finally this one smallest little *Who* who contributes just enough noise to get the message through.

Well, I'm struck by the many ways that the Horton story seems to follow many of the points made in our passage from 1 John—or John Number "Wan," as it's sometimes knawn. Horton himself gives us at least two elephantine lessons, it seems to me. The last of these lessons is the one that needs to come first nowadays. And this lesson appears when Horton says of the world of the Whos:

> "Their whole world was saved by the Smallest of All!"

Well, good grief! Who else is called the savior of the world? John puts it this way: "We . . ." We who? . . . "We *Whos*", I think would be a good way of expressing it.

> We have seen for ourselves . . . that the Father sent the Son to be the saviour of the world.
>
> (1 John 4:14 NEB)

So the savior of the world is Who Christ is, and those who have "seen it" are *Whos* in much the same way as the word "Christians" means "little Christs." And let's not forget that the savior of the world is the savior of *the world*. "Their whole world was saved," Horton says. And not *will* be saved or *can* be saved, but "*was* saved," he says. The salvation Christ brought is finished, completed—it's an already accomplished fact. If "the Father sent the Son to be the savior of the world," that's exactly what has happened and exactly who he is—he's *already* the world's savior. The *Whos* are simply the ones who have now already recognized this, but at the end of the story *everyone* will come over to their side and see it with them—"TOO!" Said the big kangaroo:

> "And, from now on, you know what I'm planning to
>   do? . . .
> From now on, I'm going to protect them with you!"
> And the young kangaroo in her pouch said, . . .
> ". . . ME, TOO!"

So "their whole world was saved by the Smallest of All!" And did not Christ identify himself with "the Smallest of All," as— for example—when he could say:

> Truly, I say to you, as you did it to one of the least of these
> my brethren, you did it to me.
>
> (Matt. 25:40 RSV)

Horton gives us a second elephantine lesson when he first hears the terrified but tiny voice of the little *Who*-ville Mayor. Horton then says:

> I'll just have to save him. Because after all,
> "A person's a person, no matter how small."

But now what *is* a "person" . . . after all . . . no matter how small? To say that "a person's a person" still doesn't really define what a person is. For a thing is defined by that thing's end, its ultimate purpose or destination, as the word *de-fine* shows us. We need to know what a person is finally *for*—that person's *fin-al* goal or *fin-ish*.

Well, *Per* is a Latin prefix that often means "for." For instance, when we say *per annum* or *per diem*, we mean "for the year" or "for the day." So if you'll pardon a little Seussian play-ing with the flexible English language, *person* means "for the Son." For Whom? For the Son, that's Whom! That's what all of us have been made for. We have all been created in the image of God, and that means we have all been created for the Son or for Christ. We're only complete when Christ is completely within us. So for John, a person is either a totally *full* or else a totally *empty* "God container":

> God himself dwells in us if we love one another; his love is brought to perfection within us.
>
> (1 John 4:12 NEB)

To be created in God's image means that God's image is in all of us; we are all created with a Christ-shaped image or hollow place at our centers or hearts, making us all either potential or fulfilled "God-containers." This is what a person is. And all of us are this no matter how small. Meanwhile, the merely potential God-containers are of this . . .

> . . . world, and so therefore is their teaching; that is why the world listens to them. (1 John 4:5 NEB)

Or, as our story puts it, the Wickersham Brothers—

> snatched Horton's clover! They carried it off
> To a black-bottomed eagle named Vlad Vlad-i-koff,
> A mighty strong eagle, of very swift wing,
> And they said, "Will you kindly get rid of this thing?"

—which Vlad then proceeded to do.

On the other hand, *Whos* . . .

> . . . belong to God, and a man who knows God listens to us, while he who does not belong to God refuses us a hearing.
>
> (1 John 4:6 NEB)

And speaking of "refusing us a hearing":

> The Wickersham Brothers came shouting, "What rot!
> This elephant's talking to *Whos* who are *not!*"

"What rot!/ This elephant's talking to *Whos* who are not!"? Sounds just like Paul's description of who Christians (and who *Whos*) are

God chose what is low and despised in the world, *things that are not,* to reduce to nothing things that are.

(1 Cor. 1:28 NRSV; emphasis added)

But now let's return to Horton's first mammoth observation: "Their whole world was saved by the Smallest of All!" And we said that the salvation of the whole world, just like the salvation in this story, has already been accomplished. OK. But doesn't this leave Christians, or *Whos,* with a little too much freedom if they've already been saved? Aren't we now free to "get away with anything" since we have now been assured that God has already forgiven us for everything way in advance? Yes, we are already forgiven. Yes, the whole world has already been saved. But then how do we know that this incredible good news is really true? Answer: we only know it when we show it. Or:

There's no way anyone can know this good news is true
Without obeying Jesus as Lord in whatever we do.
(Dr. Short)

Or, to use one more Seussian-type rhyme:

That all are saved is only known
By following Jesus as Lord alone. (Dr. Short)

Or, to go back to our passage from John:

If God thus loved us, dear friends, we in turn are bound to love one another.

(1 John 4:11 NEB)

But why does it follow that if God loves us then we must "in turn love one another"? Because, as John also says, if you don't show it, then you don't really know it. John's actual words are—

Everyone who loves is a child of God and knows God, but the unloving know nothing of God.

(1 John 4:8 NEB)

The assurance of God's unconditional love for all persons has been given to us once and for all through Christ. But there's this one strange thing about God's love: don't show it and you won't know it. Ultimately, "when the roll is called up yonder," every "person" will know this love—even Vlad Vlad-i-koff and the Wickersham Brothers. But right now, in this lifetime, there's no way we can know this love unless we show this love. So this is why, dear friends, even though you may be the smallest *Who* in the story, or what you have to give may be the smallest gift, your smallest action is always hugely important, not only to others but to yourself as well.

> Finally, at last! From that speck on that clover
> *Their voices were heard!* They rang out clear and clean.
> And the elephant smiled. "Do you see what I mean? . . .
> They've proven they ARE persons, no matter how small.
> And their whole world was saved by the Smallest of All!"

And that, dear friends, is the Good News for You Through *Horton Hears a Who!*

Notes

1. Joachim Jeremias, *Rediscovering the Parables* (New York: Charles Scribner's Sons, 1966), 23.

10

The Job of All Christians Is to Always Tell People, Near and Far, Just How Lucky We Are!

Deeply carved into the massive stone masonry that surrounds the top floor of a large public library, are the names of literary and philosophical giants of the ages.

Photo courtesy of Robert Short

And what to our wondering eyes should appear
Right there
Between Plato and Shakespeare?
Why, I deduce it's Dr. Seuss!—
Bringing light into the night![1] (Dr. Short)

Mercy! What is there about the work of this man that can raise his name to such impressive heights?

To answer this question we must first understand just what kind of doctor Dr. Seuss is. A PhD—a doctor of philosophy? No—although at one time he'd hoped to be a PhD. An MD—a medical doctor? Nope. I can only guess how many *honorary* doctorates Dr. Seuss—or Ted Geisel—may have accumulated during his lifetime. No doubt a whole drawer full! But that's beside the point. Because the point is that Dr. Seuss is a doctor of the soul, a doctor of wisdom, or a healer of the heart. So I don't think it would be stretching things too far if we thought of Dr. Seuss as a sort of "spiritual cardiologist," a doctor whose work can work on many levels and with many different types of people.

Did Dr. Seuss think of his work as directed toward the human heart as well as the head? Why couldn't he? As a young man attending the Episcopal church of his mother, the Lutheran church of his father, later involved in the Methodist Church, and still later attending regular chapel services while a student at Dartmouth College and Oxford University, there's no reason why Theodor Seuss Geisel could not have been familiar with some pretty heavy theological thoughts and themes. But if this were the case, why didn't he tell us up front that he had these kind of thoughts and concerns? Maybe it was because Ted Geisel was an artist, and artists generally keep their ideas to themselves, letting their art speak for them. Otherwise why be an artist if one is going to defeat the powerful effect of indirect or artistic communication by allowing direct communication to give away all of art's captivating mystery? In any case, we are told that Ted Geisel "worked absolutely alone, not influenced by anybody, doing only what he wanted."[2] So who is to say that Dr. Seuss doesn't really belong somewhere between Plato and Shakespeare?

For me, Dr. Seuss's 1973 story *Did I Ever Tell You How Lucky You Are?*, is one of his most meaningful and memorable parables. And this is because it's always (that is, at all times and in all the ways we can imagine) the job of all Christians to tell all people, near and far, just how lucky we are. This is why Christians are brought into the world in the first place. They are placed here to help bring this light into the darkness. A good example of this first-things-first approach would be the first part of Paul's letter to his fellow Christians in Ephesus. Paul has hardly had time to write "Dear Ephesians" before he gets down to business by reminding them in no uncertain terms just how lucky they are. "God", he says—

> . . . has bestowed on us in Christ every spiritual blessing in the heavenly realms. In Christ he chose us before the world was founded, to be dedicated, to be without blemish in his sight, to be full of love; and he destined us—such was his will and pleasure—to be accepted as his sons through Jesus Christ, that the glory of his gracious gift, so graciously bestowed on us in his Beloved, might redound to his praise. For in Christ our release is secured and our sins are forgiven through the shedding of his blood. Therein lies the richness of God's free grace lavished upon us imparting full wisdom and insight. He has made known to us his hidden purpose —such was his will and pleasure determined beforehand in Christ—to be put into effect when the time was ripe: namely, that the universe, all in heaven and on earth, might be brought into a unity in Christ.
>
> In Christ indeed we have been given our share in the heritage, as was decreed in his design whose purpose is everywhere at work. For it was his will that we, who were the first to set our hope on Christ, should cause his glory to be praised. And you too, when you had heard the message of the truth, the good news of your salvation, and had believed it, became incorporate in Christ and received the seal of the

promised Holy Spirit; and that Spirit is the pledge that we shall enter upon our heritage, when God has redeemed what is his own, to his praise and glory.

(Eph. 1:3–14 NEB)

Friends, that's not just telling Christians *how* lucky they are, but it's also telling them *why* they're so all-fired lucky! And it seems to me that *Did I Ever Tell You How Lucky You Are?* is following pretty much the same theme and arguments.

The story opens with a scene between its two principals, a young guy and an old guy, in the midst of a huge, lonely wasteland, the old guy sitting atop a tall cactus. The old guy, "with a sunny sweet smile on his face," sings:

> When you think things are bad,
> when you feel sour and blue,
>
> . . . .
> Just tell yourself, Duckie,
> you're really quite lucky!
> Some people are much more . . .
> unlucky than you!

And then the following twenty-one scenes are beautifully designed to show us in wildly colorful, creative, and funny ways just how unlucky some people and various other creatures can be. If Samuel Beckett was right when he said, "Nothing is funnier than unhappiness," then this truth can explain why all of these postcards from hell are so funny. "It's a troublesome world," Dr. Seuss begins by showing and telling us. . . .

> You ought to be thankful, a whole heaping lot,
> for the places and people you're lucky you're not!

Then examples, like living in "Ga-Zayt" and getting caught in traffic on "Zayt Highway Eight." Or Ali Sard's mowing his uncle's quick-growing grass that grows as he mows it. Or having a tail full of unsolvable knots. Or trying to teach Irish ducks how to read Jivvanese. And so on and on, with the scenes gradually getting darker and more menacing in color, outlook, and design. The next to last picture shows a gloomy, almost frightening empty landscape, where we are told:

> Thank goodness you're not something someone forgot,
> and left all alone in some punkerish place
> like a rusty tin coat hanger hanging in space.

But the whole story ends happily and in bright colors with the young guy also sitting on top a cactus and now also "with a sunny sweet smile on his face." And his old friend brings down the curtain by telling him:

> That's why I say "Duckie!
> Don't grumble! Don't stew!
> Some critters are much-much . . .
> more unlucky than you!"

That's it! That's Dr. Seuss's *Did I Ever Tell You How Lucky You Are?* And now for the message of the gospel, the good news, which says exactly the same thing to us: "Did I ever tell you how lucky you are?"

First, "how lucky you *are!*" Not what kind of luck you may have today or tomorrow. The gospel is far more interested in how lucky you *are*—period! How lucky you are *permanently*, now and forever, "in the great scheme of things," "in the eyes of eternity." And the gospel tells us that in the eyes of eternity we are all infinitely lucky!

How so? First, it was God's decision not only to give us our lives here and now but far more than that to give us all eternal life—"all this and heaven too," for each and every one of us. People often respond to this aspect of how lucky we are by saying, "I wish I could believe that!" Well, if they really would like to believe this good news they certainly have the New Testament to back it up. For instance, in the above passage from Ephesians, Paul assures us (in another translation) that

> [God] has let us know the mystery of his purpose, according to his good pleasure which he determied beforehand in

Christ, for him to act upon when the times had run their
course: that he would bring everything together under
Christ, as head, everything in the heavens and everything
on earth.

(Eph. 1:9–10 NJB)

That's infinitely lucky, Duckie! But then there's more—plenty
more! For God is not going to "make known" this wonderfully
perfect final outcome for all of us without also giving us the
means of now knowing for sure that this good news is really
true. And this God does for us when we follow—or believe
in—the risen Christ and then experience the resulting heartfelt
confirmation of all of this by the comforting presence of
Christ's spirit, the Holy Spirit. "And you too," Duckie,

when you had heard the message of the truth, the good
news of your salvation, and had believed it, became incor-
porate in Christ and received the seal of the promised Holy
Spirit; and that Spirit is the pledge that we shall enter upon
our heritage, when God has redeemed what is his own, to
his praise and glory.

(Eph. 1:13–14 NEB)

Now that's lucky! But there's even more, Duckie! For what
about the "sunny sweet smiles" on their faces that both the old
guy and the young guy end up with, even while they sit in "terribly prickly places"? Can it be that even prickly places can be
seen as being lucky for us? Why, sure! For it's in the very nature
of our luckiness that Christ is given to us as the way to know
God and his unconditional love for all people, and "prickly
places"—our crosses, our suffering—are given to us as the doorway to knowing Christ. We come to know Christ through our
need—through the "prickly places."

But then there's "how *lucky* you are!"—"lucky" in the sense
that all of this could have been vastly different. All of the wonderful things that God has given us are gifts, not anything we
deserve or have earned or just naturally have coming to us. This

is why the New Testament is so anxious that we understand that we only live by God's grace. Even our faith in God, even our "good deeds" for God, are gifts from God:

> For it is by grace you are saved through faith; it is not your own doing. It is God's gift, not a reward for work done. There is nothing for anyone to boast of; we are God's hand-iwork, created in Christ Jesus for the life of good deeds which God designed for us.
>
> (Eph. 2:8–10 REB)

In other words, you're just *lucky*, Duckie. It is death to the spirit to think that our salvation is something that we can in any way achieve for ourselves, in which case we become our own saviors. Either Christ is our savior or else we are. We can't have it both ways.

"Thank goodness for all the things you are not," Dr. Seuss's old guy ends up saying to his young guy. And indeed, most of this book consists of Hieronymus Bosch–like pictures of poor hell-trapped sufferers who are much more unlucky than us. But what could be the point of Dr. Seuss emphasizing all of these poor "unlucky" folks? As we said earlier, part of the point is the funnyness of unhappiness. But is there more? Must our happiness be the result of others being so unhappy and our remembering how unhappy they are?

Well, what's the point of "hell" in the New Testament, espe-cially after all we know through Christ about God's final salva-tion of *all* people? First of all, hell is in the New Testament to describe the *present* predicament of people who don't know how lucky they are; and second, it's there to remind us one more time of how lucky we are: God doesn't have to save all people. God doesn't *have* to save anyone. God could have been some other kind of God, like the terrible God who creates the trap and then creates people with the strong tendency to go into the trap, and then leaves them there like "something some-one forgot." And, mind you, Duckie, there are plenty of reli-gious groups, including many that call themselves "Christian," that believe just that! God could have been the kind of God who could easily decide to send you to hell for all eternity! And we have no right to take God's choice in this matter for granted. Nevertheless, the God of Jesus didn't choose to be this kind of kindless God. For through Christ we know that in Christ

> the complete being of God, by God's own choice, came to dwell. Through him God chose to reconcile the whole universe to himself, making peace through the shedding of his blood upon the cross—to reconcile all things, whether on earth or in heaven, through him alone.
>
> (Col. 1:19–20 NEB)

So just remember to remember, Duckie, how lucky you are! You and everyone else with you!

Has anyone ever told you this—how lucky you are? Well, they should, because this is "the message of the truth, the good news of your salvation" (Eph. 1:13 NEB). And telling people this is not optional for Christians, something they can do or not do as they please: "For it was his will that we, who already enjoyed the hope of Christ, should cause his glory to be praised" (Eph. 1:12 NEB, variant reading).

And this is really *news*; it's not anything we can just wishfully think up and tell ourselves. Like all that's really new, it's not anything we just naturally already know; therefore, it must always come from outside-in. Everyone needs to be *told* this news.

And it's always *good* news too, not just partially good, or good for some people but not for others. This is why the gospel message itself, the good news as it's addressed to all people, will always sound exactly like this: "Did I ever tell you how lucky you are?"

> So what do you know? This story contains the good neuss
> According to the New Testament *and* Dr. Seuss!
> (Dr. Short)

Notes

1. Main Library, Little Rock, Arkansas.

2. Judith and Neil Morgan, *Dr. Seuss and Mr. Geisel* (New York: Random House, 1995), 223.

11

Bartholomew and the Oobleck

Or

Dr. Seuss and the Church

The story of *Bartholomew and the Oobleck* can easily be seen as Dr. Seuss's view of what the church should look like. It should decidedly be "low" and "protestant." That is, it should be humble, plain, and simple. And it should not hanker after anything more than what God originally gave it. But hanker the King did in this story, not being satisfied with "the sky's" original gifts of rain, sunshine, fog, and snow, "these four things," the King said, "that come down from my sky." The King wanted "something NEW to come down!" And so "the-King-Got-Angry-with-the-Sky."

The King then calls in his "royal magicians" and demands that they make "something fall from my skies that no other kingdom has ever had before." The magicians, "mystic men" all looking identical in their long robes and high hats, also speak together in a kind of magical-mystical chant. They promise the King to have the sky send down "oobleck," which is so new that they don't even know what it is themselves. The King's magicians chant:

"Oh, snow and rain are not enough!
Oh, we must make some brand-new stuff!"

The King is delighted with this prospect, but his young page boy, Bartholomew Cubbins (Bartholomew is the name of one of Christ's twelve Apostles) is frightened by what the magicians' "terrible magic" might end up producing. And so Bartholomew the protestant protests against the whole idea.

Nevertheless, the King's wish is granted and oobleck begins to fall, at first slowly but soon the entire kingdom is covered with it. Oobleck is a kind of green goo that gums up and sticks to everything it touches, including the now helpless King.

"Fetch my magicians, Bartholomew!" the King frantically commands. "Make them say some magic words! Make them stop the oobleck falling!" But Bartholomew can't do this because the magicians' "cave on Mountain Neeka-tave is buried deep in oobleck." Finally—

> Bartholomew Cubbins could hold his tongue no longer.
> "And (the oobleck is) going to keep on falling," he shouted, "until your whole great marble palace tumbles down! So don't waste your time saying foolish *magic* words. YOU ought to be saying some plain *simple* words!"
> "*Simple* words . . . ? What do you mean, boy?"
> "I mean" said Bartholomew, "this is all *your* fault! Now, the least you can do is say the simple words, 'I'm sorry'."
> No one had ever talked to the King like this before.

"I *am* sorry!" sobs the King. "I'm awfully, a*wfully* sorry!" Then the oobleck stopped falling and "just simply, quietly melted away."

No "miracle, mystery and authority" (to use the words of Dostoevsky's "Grand Inquisitor" in *The Brothers Karamazov*), but only simplicity, plainness and humility, and being quite content with what the church was originally given by its Lord. Sure looks like the New Testament church to me!

Or as Shakespeare (like Seuss, another Low Church Protestant) could say in words that apply equally well to the Christian church, to Christian faith, and to Dr. Seuss's *Bartholomew and the Oobleck:*

Ever note . . .
When love begins to sicken and decay,
It useth an enforced ceremony.
There are no tricks in plain and simple faith.
               (*Julius Caesar*, 4.2.19–22)

In looking back over this book, I was startled to see how often Shakespeare is mentioned. Won't Shakespeare's name seem strangely out of place, I wondered? But then I remembered what the Morgans tell us in their biography when Ted ("Dr. Seuss") Geisel is discussing a pet project with a close friend:

> Ted talked with him about a *Cat in the Hat* read-aloud anthology, a collection of forty-two of Ted's favorite tales for children by authors including A. A. Milne, Carl Sandburg, Lewis Carroll, William Shakespeare and Jesus Christ.[1]

No, I concluded. Shakespeare won't be out of place at all.

Notes

1. Judith and Neil Morgan, *Dr. Seuss and Mr. Geisel: A Biography* (New York: Random House, 1995), 202.

CPSIA information can be obtained at www.ICGtesting.com
Printed in the USA
LVOW08s0323041115

460985LV00003B/126/P